A Sweet Life

A Sweet Life

Growing up in a
Dorset sweet shop

LUCINDA OSMOND

COPPER
KETTLE
PRESS

COPPER KETTLE PRESS

For Pa

Clive Osmond, Pa, completing the first Dorchester Lions
Fun Run in 1982. As a member of Dorchester Lions,
he took up running to take part in this event,
later completing marathons in London, Paris and Berlin.

Black Magic & Flying Saucers

I GREW UP in a sweet shop, the kind that doesn't exist any more, and if I close my eyes I can actually smell it. The sugariness of coconut ice, Turkish delight and vanilla fudge blended with the organic mellowness of pipe tobacco. I can hear the door opening and closing with its accompanying bell. I can see the cheerful faces of the children on their Saturday morning ritual, here to spend their pocket money. They are always in such a desperate hurry, as if the money is burning a hole in their pocket. The pre-school children are accompanied, often with their dads, to help with the tricky process of putting a wriggly, chewy snake into a white paper bag. So hard to choose from Black Jacks and Fruit Salad Chews, Catherine Wheels and Sherbet Fountains, chocolate mice and sweet bananas, flying saucers, fizz bombs and bubble gum. The older kids feast in swarms arriving altogether and packing out the shop. But they'll be quick, knowing what they want, and then they'll be gone.

I can see the highly polished shine on the chocolate covered peanuts and the bright opalescence of hard boiled sweets. And my dad, whom we called Pa, chatting with customers, weighing out wine gums, doing sums in his head. I can see the gleaming chrome of the conch-shaped scales reflecting the gem-coloured wrappers of Quality Street. But most of all I sense optimism, adventure and fun.

What smelt special, felt magical, was normal; was my home.

But where are the farmers in their patched-up Barbours? Where are the wives in their Dax and Hebe tweed carrying wicker baskets of vegetables from the barrows up the street? What has happened to the council men in their donkey jackets and hobnail boots, smelling of creosote hot from the road, holding out nicotine-stained fingers of cash for an ounce of Old Holborn? What of the lawyers buying humbugs to see them through court, or the nuns buying mints after Mass? Where are the Hardye schoolboys buying tuck to last them the week or the Romanies with bad teeth, and clothes smelling of woodsmoke? Where are the customers dressed up for the evening, popping in before closing, for a box of Black Magic for the dinner party host? And where are the grimacing faces of the psychiatric patients, dosed up on Largactil, struggling to say the word 'peppermint'? Do people like that even exist any more?

What we did felt important. It might have been just jelly babies to the onlooker, but it was so much more than that. People relied on us every day. It felt special to be part of their daily or weekly routine, a fleeting yet frequent encounter. They were as much a part of our lives as we were of theirs, and we liked it like that.

People whose names we knew came in as regular as sunrise for their sweets and their smokes. Where have they gone?

I had returned to the shop that we had run, our family enterprise. I stood on the pavement outside, looking up and down the street. It felt narrower, ordinary. I looked up at the flat above our shop where we had lived for the first few years, the bedrooms at the very top, the lounge and kitchen on the second floor. The double sash windows of our lounge, where Grandma would sit on carnival day in her best summer dress and silk headscarf watching the floats go by; the room where my sister Caroline had her sixth birthday party, hosted by the magician who lived above the shoe shop across the road. I recall the photo of her in her puffball dress with eyes as large and red as the rabbit's, fighting back the streaming nose and urge to sneeze, sitting still and stoic, determined to cradle a rabbit 'out of a hat' on her special day. And the corner, where we placed our Christmas tree, not real, not back then, but a 1970s showpiece of shimmering silver foil.

And the two bedroom windows at the top, Caroline's on the left, which she nearly fell out of one day. The manager of Curry's, opposite, ran over to alert Pa that she was precariously hanging out. Pa bounded like David Hemery up the stairs and pulled her back, unhitching her from the loop of barbed wire on the sill put there to keep off the pigeons. We had had a rare childish spat, she and I, and as I slammed her door, the spare mattress leaning against the wall outside her bedroom slid down like a blanket of snow and blocked her exit so that she couldn't get out. She had been leaning out the second storey window calling 'Daddy, Daddy!' hoping that he would hear her, working in the shop below.

It seems strange to think that we lived and slept on the main shopping street. There are no houses here, only shops. Our front door was the shop door, there was no other entrance or exit. When we moved in and moved out, all our furniture passed through here. Our groceries, our post, everything, came in through the shop door. This is where we stood ready to leave for school, satchels in hand, and where we returned at the end of the day.

How small the building looked, – did we really have our shop here? It is a clothes shop now, the frontage completely changed, the old wooden window frames and brass handled door replaced with double-glazed uniformity. And of course, the name above reading *Osmond's Tobacconist & Confectioner, Cards & Gifts*, all gone.

I went to go inside but I couldn't. It felt like I was pushing against a forcefield. I couldn't get through it. My heart beat faster and it was hard to breathe. I wanted to cry. I was buffeted back out onto the street, so I stopped to take a few deep breaths before bracing myself for another attempt.

As I tried again, I became aware of the receding backdrop of ladies' clothes as the bright colours and smell of our shop came to the fore. I was transported back in time, walking in as if just back from school, seeing Pa serving a customer, weighing out sweets in a white paper bag, smiling at me as I came through the door. Looking around I saw the red marble-effect lino, the shelves of heavy glass jars, the displays of sweets and chocolate bars, stacks of cigarettes, tins of tobacco and boxes of fudge. I had assumed that, with the shop gone, and it looking so completely different, it would not feel the same. How could it? But like returning to your childhood home, you can still feel your connection with it despite the new owner's alterations.

And a lot had been altered. All that remained of the cellar stairs was a trap door in the floor. We had stored the sweets and tobacco down there. The cellar was an integral part of the shop for us. It was closed off now, its steep narrow steps no doubt assessed a safety hazard. It had been sealed off like stoppering an empty perfume bottle, but pull out the bung and the essence would surely still be there.

As I walked back down the street I could see how much had changed, the town had been changing and so had I. While the town had been losing its individuality, I had been gaining mine.

I thought it was lost forever, the part we played in the shop, 'all dead and gone', as my grandmother used to say. I thought it had died with Pa. But clearly it hadn't. Like finding treasure on a wreck beneath the waves, just because it has been forgotten doesn't mean it's not there.

2

(Bed &) Breakfast at Tiffany's

I DON'T THINK either of my parents ever meant to run a sweet shop. Their career ambitions were much more traditional, Pa's to be an engineer and Ma's to be a nurse. Pa worked as a draughtsman, designing torpedoes at AUWE (Admiralty Underwater Weapons Establishment) on Portland near Weymouth, arriving not long after two employees were found guilty of selling secrets to the KGB.

Although his job at the Admiralty could have been a job for life, Pa soon realised that the only way to get promoted was for his boss either to retire or die. Either way he could have a long wait. Pa was offered promotion in Scotland. When he got to his interview in the new town of East Kilbride, he was surprised to find that questions focused on why he wanted to move north, when everyone there was trying to move south. It was a town of shift workers, husbands and wives passing each other in the night. When Ma stopped to ask a woman with a pushchair what it was like living there, the woman looked her up and down and said, 'Looking at you, dear, you wouldn't like it here.'

Pa turned down the promotion, had his overtime cut, and was no longer able to afford to live in the 1960s new-build they had bought as newly-weds. It was an aspirational dream they couldn't afford. Ma sold her wedding dress to pay the electricity bill, and they put their house on the market and moved on. 'Never look back,' has always been Ma's philosophy, 'sometimes you need to go backwards in order to go forwards.' It was time to heed her own advice.

We moved to a guest house a couple of miles from Weymouth seafront. As Ma had stepped out of her nursing career after having children she thought taking over this business would be a good way to supplement Pa's income. I was about five, my sister Caroline, three. Our guest house, Tiffany's, was a six-bedroomed Victorian villa with a leaking roof, rising damp and a tower with a ghost. I still remember the bucket at the end of my bed to collect the drips. It was a house of interesting smells, the mustiness of dry rot combined with the sweetness of hops from my father's often explosive attempts at home-brew.

The tower we took for granted. Didn't every house have one? The entrance was through a narrow door at the end of the landing and up the carpeted stairs, rain-soaked and curled up at the edges, crispy to the touch. Caroline and I used to open the little window onto the gulley between the two sloped roofs and crawl out hoping we might see the sea. But we never got far. It felt scary, and anyway there wasn't much to look at because of the steep pitch of the roof. Our resolve would soon fade and we would make our retreat back down the stairs.

Tiffany's ghost was seen by Ma several times on the landing near the entrance to the tower. The ghost was of a lady, with hair in a bun, wearing a white-collared grey crinoline dress. She looked at Ma and smiled, then disappeared.

After we sold Tiffany's the new owner asked Ma one day if she had ever 'seen anything'. The new owner said that she had seen a woman in a grey dress, and heard the rustle of a crinoline skirt on the landing. Her young son had seen something too. One day when he had been at home ill, she went to offer him a drink of water only to be told that, 'Someone's just given me a drink, a lady in a grey dress.' We learned later that two actress sisters had lived in the house in Victorian times. Perhaps our mysterious visitor was one of them.

The garden felt huge, even in the front, set out in a square with a path all around where we could ride our bike and trike. Hanging bells of fuchsias, snapdragons and foxgloves in pinks and purples flourished in the herbaceous borders. Ma did it all – I don't know where she found the time, but it was a source of pure joy for her. We had a vegetable patch at the back and even as a youngster I did my bit digging it over, although I was more interested in the pieces of blue and white pottery it produced than the runner beans we were planting.

In the summer months, Weymouth attracted day-trippers and holidaymakers, as now, enjoying the safe sandy beach and picturesque bay. We had donkey rides, Victorian-style fairground swings and trampolines right on the beach. The guests were mostly factory workers from Wales or the Midlands, coming in Wakes week, the last week of July or first week of August when the factories closed. It was the women who saved up for the holiday via their thrift club and paid in cash when they left.

A couple called the Morgans, who used to return to us each year, explained why they kept on coming back. 'I come to Dorset to lie in a field and listen to the cricket; the missus does her knitting. Living in a high-rise flat and hearing the lift going all night long, for me this is Paradise.'

In the winter Ma took in students from the local teacher training college. Aside from providing board and lodging Ma was a combination of agony aunt and boarding school matron, listening and dispensing advice to the young women living away from home for the first time.

Running a guest house in the 1960s was a tough business, particularly without the essential luxury of modern day appliances. Having fourteen guests living in your home, being dependent on you for bed, breakfast and evening meal, is wearing when you have neither dishwasher nor washing machine. The washing-up used to take forever.

Theirs was a team effort, Ma being in charge of breakfasts and changing the beds, and Pa coming home to help with the evening meal when he got back from work. Dinner was served at 6pm and Pa would be back in time to make and serve the starter. On the occasions when a prisoner had escaped from Portland Prison and Pa's journey had been delayed by police roadblocks, the guests would have to make do with a glass of fruit juice as a starter instead.

We sometimes had people turning up at the house ad hoc, desperate for a bed for the night. One such was a man who had missed the ferry to Jersey, and said he would sleep anywhere. All the rooms were taken so Ma offered him the lounge floor. In the hall was an old blanket box that had come with the house. It had unusually ornate hinges and a big black key. 'Never get rid of that,' he said to Ma as he left early in the morning, 'that's worth a few bob.' When we came to sell up, Ma got the most reputable antiques dealer in the area to value the box. He said it was only worth about a hundred pounds. It was very heavy to move and there was no room for it where we going, so it was left behind. The new owners of Tiffany's later sold it for two thousand pounds.

One day Pa noticed the floorboards in the lounge were warped. On closer inspection he realised that the supporting joists were rotten. There was also the strangely distinctive smell of Yardley soap. Just at that moment, a guest in the upstairs bathroom emptied the bath, and a stream of frothy scented water coursed its way between the joists. So not only was there the leaking roof and rising damp, but the floorboards were rotten too. Tiffany's was turning out to be a bigger money drain than my parents had anticipated. It was time to move on again.

And that's when they heard that the local goldmine was up for sale.

3

Torpedoes – Lethal to Liquorice

T HE GOLDMINE WAS a sweet shop in Dorchester. It was an established business in a prime location, in the eye of the needle between Marks & Spencer and Boots the chemist, and it presented a great opportunity. But it would be hard. The shop was open all hours from 8am to 9pm, seven days a week, and we would have to go and live in the flat above it, a flat that had no garden.

It was a very big step for Pa to give up his job and move us to Dorchester. He would sit for hours going over his calculations, trying to work out the likely income. And then there was the unknown. You never knew how much success was down to personality. Could they make it work?

They decided it was worth a go. Pa wanted to get on. He couldn't wait any longer for his boss to retire, he wanted to work for himself. However, not everyone was behind him. His father sent him pleading letters not to take the risk, not to waste his education, to stick to what he knew. He advised him against turning his back on his prestigious career as an engineer. But I have learned from Pa that sometimes you've just got to go for it. Do your sums, trust your gut and get out there and try. Very rarely is there no path back. People around you may be scared for you but you can't let their fears put you off. They don't have your perspective and may not have your drive.

So, on a winter's day in 1970 we went to take our very first look at the sweet shop. Mrs Walker, the vendor proprietor, gave my sister and me the task of breaking up trays of toffee with little metal hammers while my parents talked business in the flat above the shop. She was a confident woman, highly perfumed and coiffed with immaculate manicures and pencilled-in brows. Her husband, a little stooped, was a man who looked like he couldn't wait for his retirement to start. Pa remarked afterwards that the bell on the shop door was ringing so much, he thought there must have been someone ringing it to make the shop sound busy. The next thing I knew we were settling ourselves into the flat, making our home above a sweet shop. It was 1971, I was six years old, and Osmond's Tobacconist & Confectioner was born.

Our shop, at 51 South Street, stood proud at the end of a short terrace of other shops, close to the front of the pavement. The bank and businesses further along were set back from the road as if they were more timid about speaking to their customers. Above the shop on each floor were a pair of large sash windows topped with red patterned brickwork giving them the appearance of wide open doll's eyes.

Although it had been a sweet shop for some years before we took it over, back in the 1930s it had been a tea room, and the bread ovens were still in the cellar. Although they were boarded up behind wooden panels it wasn't difficult to imagine a baker in a chef's hat and floured apron bringing out trays of warm pastries and bread to the delight of customers. A 1936 trade directory lists the tea and dining rooms of pastry cook and confectioner C.H. Stroud, and there is a ghost sign, the remains of a painted advertisement on the wall outside that reads *Stroud, Confectioner, Restaurateur, Dining Rooms*. I have met people who used to go there with their mums for a treat as a child and be served pretty cakes on patterned china by waitresses in starched uniforms. Sometime after it had been a tea room, the premises of 51 South Street was actually run as two distinct shops, being split in two from front to back. The other half of our shop was a greengrocers run by Mrs Walker's son, Ron.

Both shops had their own identical doorways of a fully glazed door with brass bar placed diagonally across it. Pushing firmly on the bar of our door rang the bell at the top to alert us to the arrival of a customer. Despite its small size, customers seemed perfectly prepared to queue outside, which they often did, especially on market day and Saturdays.

I have never been in another shop like ours. Apart from its size, it was quite unusual. We didn't have a counter to stand behind as the sweet displays were arranged all around the edge of the shop. We stood with our customers in the shop, the only difference being that we faced outwards and the customers faced in. On the left-hand side as you entered was an entire wall of sweets, the weigh-out sweets, as we called them, that we sold by the quarter or half pound. These were displayed in Perspex boxes tilted downwards so that the customers could see what was inside. Some of the bestsellers were rainbow drops – little chocolate pastilles coated in hundreds and thousands – or chewy milk gums in the shape of milk bottles, or toasted teacakes – little gummy coconut roasted morsels like mini muffins. We sold tons of chocolate buttons in white or dark chocolate and chewing nuts, though these were not to be recommended for people with dentures or loose fillings. Above was a high shelf bearing heavy glass jars of Murray Mints, Pear Drops, Creamline Toffees, and many more, and above that another shelf busy with boxes of chocolates. We had Black Magic, Milk Tray, Terry's All Gold, or for something less expensive, Matchmakers, which looked like chocolate flavoured Twiglets. My favourite were Neapolitans, individually wrapped rectangles of chocolate in mocha, orange or café au lait.

On the right-hand side of the shop was a dark oak unit displaying chocolate bars. We stocked Cadbury's Dairy Milk or Fruit and Nut in every size from the smallest to the largest, Bar Six, Toffee Crisp, Picnic, Curlywurly, Topic, Caramac and the blue shiny wrapper of Ice Breaker with its crunchy minty pieces, and the rum and raisin flavour of Old Jamaica reminiscent of the smugglers of *Moonfleet*. Underneath the bars of chocolate was a lower shelf, at child's eye level for the Saturday morning sweet buying ritual.

You could see the playful delight in the eyes of customers at the freedom to choose a quarter of wine gums over chocolate eclairs. The fun was in the choosing then disappearing out of the door and down the street with a white paper bag of sweets in their hand to eat, share, or keep for another day. It was a delicate balance between offering customers 'their usual' and teasing them with the new releases, new lines of confectionery or speciality chocolates. Our customers had varied tastes and we did our best to satisfy their requests. 'Mr Osmond, have you got any of those glacé fruits like they have on the telly?' someone might ask. I would watch as Pa, who had never had a day's customer service training in his life, tear off a large paper bag and write 'Special Order' with the pencil from behind his ear, as he made a note to speak to the rep to get them in for next week.

Not long after we moved to the shop, I turned seven, celebrating my birthday in a most grown-up way. Pa and I had lunch together in the Chinese restaurant next door, surrounded by red paper lanterns and flock wallpaper. I suppose Ma was minding the shop and my sister. We were the only people eating there. It was just the second time I had ever eaten Chinese food and I loved it. Sadly, the restaurant was on the watch list of the Public Health Department and was later closed down by the health inspectors. The family who ran it disappeared overnight leaving behind their laundry and a rotting dog carcass in the back yard that we could see from our kitchen window.

When we arrived in Dorchester every shop except for a handful was privately owned. There was a small Marks & Spencer, a Woolworths and a Boots, but apart from that all the shops were family-run. There were carpet shops, men's outfitters, leather goods shops, and tea and coffee merchants. There were several very smart ladies' dress shops with the word 'gowns' above the window. As a young teen I would go into Pamela James with Ma when she needed a new dress and she would be served by a mature lady and her assistant, both exquisitely presented and groomed to perfection. You knew you were somewhere special as soon as you set foot in the place. The impossibly impractical cream-coloured carpet and heavy brocade curtains were a throwback to an age of elegance. Just being in that shop I felt older, taller, touched by the brush of tastefulness despite my casual jeans and Donny Osmond T-shirt. It was a perfumed world of polite attention. If the shop were a sweet it would be a softly scented violet cream encased in dark chocolate served in a pleated paper wrapper; the sort of sweet to savour not scoff.

There was a chemist next door to the greengrocers that was a sanctuary of stillness. It would have been a good place to sit and read a book if it had had comfy chairs. It was very bright, the light pouring in through the orange tinted film covering the windows and reflecting off the tall apothecary jars containing coloured liquids. You would be served by a lady in a white coat, or sometimes the white-bearded pharmacist who spent most of his time out the back. Nothing was immediately at hand, everything came out of a mahogany drawer or a glass fronted cabinet. In the window was an advert for Dr Scholl's sandals, shoes which my sister and I coveted and which we eventually got Ma to buy us. It took us a few weeks to get used to walking in them, the wooden bump killing our feet to begin with. I never saw anyone else in the chemist when I went in, even though every purchase seemed to take an age. It was very different from our shop, which was hardly ever empty or silent, the bell above the door ringing all the time.

When we arrived in the town, some of the other businesses had been there for many years, some since 1895. One of these was Miles the saddlers with its life-size plaster horse in the window modelling bridles and bits, the whole shop smelling beautifully of leather. Another was Parsons, the 'grocer, tea dealer and provision merchant'. This was where customers could place their food orders to be delivered to their home. I used to go in with my grandmother who would be served by an aproned assistant behind a long wooden counter. Parsons used to roast their coffee in the shop window, the extractor fan sending the aroma out into the street. I remember that when it closed down my friends and I felt sad. It wasn't that it had played a huge part in our lives, but it felt like the end of an era, another long-standing independent shop gone. It felt a bit like when the girls in a class above me left school; it brings your time to leaving closer still. It made me realise that every business has a life span. How long would ours be?

One thing Ma and Pa both knew was that this venture would not fail through lack of effort on their part. They trusted each other completely, the one wouldn't let the other down. They were in it together and prepared to work hard. Whether it would be a success they didn't know, but they would give it a damned good go.

'With each step we burnt our bridges. We had to make it work,' Ma told me.

4

Introducing Pa

MY FATHER CLIVE, whom we called Pa, was a deeply pragmatic man, any decision-making beginning with two columns headed Pros and Cons. He was logical and sensible and probably just a bit eccentric. Or maybe that's how he became living with us. He had a practical solution for every problem we presented him with, most of which were usually met with the response, 'I've got something for that in the garage.' School boaters that blew off our heads in a gust of wind got lined with draft excluder, and his sore muscles or aching joints got sprayed with WD40. When he started applying brown wood stain to his greying beard, he replied to our bemused looks, 'Why not? It works on wood.'

Being a draughtsman he was skilled at typography, neatly labelling our satchels and geometry sets, each letter elegantly drawn and evenly spaced; no wonky letters or names running downhill for us. He was brilliant with numbers, could draw anything as long as it had straight lines, and achieved whatever he put his mind to. He took up running in his mid-forties, completing marathons in London, Paris and Berlin, and achieved a personal best of three hours fourteen minutes. Not bad for a fifty-one-year-old asthmatic.

He could mend anything, even at times improving on the design. Electrical appliances would be taken apart, their inner workings scrutinised for fault and reassembled. He would get them working again but often with a collection of parts left over. I recall the look of dismay on his face as the newly repaired Kenwood Chef sat whirring next to a random collection of orphaned springs and bolts. Such was the absolute unwavering belief in his ability to solve any problem that when the top of my four-year-old sister's finger got chopped off in the closing door of a telephone box, she declared confidently to the hospital doctor, 'Daddy will mend it.'

His workbench in the garage was his place of sanctuary, planing blocks of wood or soldering pieces of metal, wearing his old leather motor-racing goggles to protect his eyes. Dressed in his dusty overalls he would be a sight of complete contentment, perfectly at home with the smell of oil and turps as the paint-spattered radio played Radio 2 in the background. Turn up with a mug of tea and one of Ma's homemade biscuits hot from the oven and he would be as happy as Larry.

He had an amazing array of tools collected over the years, both imperial and metric. Some of them dated back to his apprenticeship as a mechanical engineer or when he used to build kit cars. When he didn't have the right tool he would make it. He maintained his garage like a chef does a kitchen, each tool immediately at hand and perfect for the job. The spanners and wrenches feeling heavy to the touch, the polished patina of wooden-handled screwdrivers and chisels worn smooth through use.

His was the era of handbrake turns and the double de-clutch. Many a time before I had learned to drive, we would return to a flat battery and he would have me steer the car while he and a willing passer-by would try to jump start it. 'Release the clutch now, Lucinda!' he would shout from behind as I did my best to strain my child-length legs to reach for the pedals. With a jolt and a splutter the engine would jerk back to life. It was fun, it was maverick, it was exciting to be part of. He loved cars, building and racing them from his teenage years. When he first started dating Ma, the Rochdale sports car he built and drove certainly added to his charm. She loved its sleek lines and doe-eyed headlights and was disappointed when he turned up next time in a brand new Mini Cooper. The shiny replacement was not to her taste, even if it was modelled by Twiggy and The Rolling Stones.

Because he had built cars he knew how they should run. He would be alert to every rattle or whistle, every thud or wheeze. As we drove along he would have me empty the glove compartment to eliminate the possible cause, his ears as alert as a bloodhound's. One day when I was about six, in the days before seat belts, I remember riding in the front passenger seat of our family car when a pedestrian stepped out suddenly into the road. Pa slammed on the brakes and thrust out his left arm in front of me, stopping me going through the windscreen.

When I was born Pa went straight down to the local newspaper office to file a birth announcement in the name of Juliet, the name he and Ma had chosen for me. He returned to the postnatal ward to tell Ma the good news. She had changed her mind, and had already written the birth announcement cards for Lucinda, the name chosen from a book she had been reading. Without any fuss, he went straight down to the *Echo* office to notify them of the change. I don't know if it was the hormones at work or Ma's romantic notion, but it does seem odd to me that she didn't discuss it with him first. What doesn't surprise me, though, is his uncomplaining response.

For my tenth birthday Pa renovated a second-hand bicycle. He stripped it back and reassembled it, oiling every cog and polishing the chrome until gleaming. He spray-painted it bluebell blue, put new white grips on the handlebars and fixed a matching saddle bag with white trim on the back. The final touch were the transfers. Compared to building and racing cars in his youth, my bike would have been a less taxing project, but he loved doing it and I watched with eager anticipation at every stage of progress. The day I was able to take it out and ride it was even better than if he had bought me a brand new bike.

When I became a teenager, hitting that tricky transition between childhood and adulthood, calling my parents Mummy and Daddy started to feel uncomfortable, but the option of Mum and Dad felt a bit plain. My parents weren't like the mums and dads I knew. They needed to be called something different. When I was applying for nurse training at London hospitals, Ma joked that she hoped I wouldn't be embarrassed by them coming to visit, up from the sticks, from Dorset. The image of them rolling up to Guy's Hospital on a lilting horse-drawn wagon like a couple of yokels came to mind, and the rural-sounding names Ma and Pa stuck.

Ma had wanted to marry a farmer, a romantic notion that didn't come off. Pa was never going to be a farmer, that was not his calling. He always said that he wanted to retire by fifty, that was his goal. Sadly, that never happened either. One of the dreams that he did get to fulfil, though, was building his own house. With his experience at the Admiralty he was familiar with architectural plans and he loved scheming and designing. Ma had noticed an advertisement in the local paper for the sale of a pocket of land out at one of the villages, Winterbourne Steepleton, but she thought it was further from the centre of Dorchester than it was. Coming across the advertisement again a few weeks later, she realised that it was actually nearby. On impulse they drove out and saw the land and quickly did a deal with the builder. Pa stayed up all night and delivered the plans for the house the next day. The builder was taken aback, saying, 'What are you, a bloody architect?' Well, he wasn't. He was just someone who was used to drawing plans. I think he thought that if he could design a torpedo, which had to move, then designing a house couldn't be that difficult.

5

Living Above the Shop

OR THE FIRST few years we lived in the flat above the shop. My bedroom overlooked the street, a heady two floors up. Heaving up the window, leaning out, I had a unique view of South Street. Twist my head to the left and I could see the Corn Exchange clock, whose chimes partitioned my sleep. Look straight ahead and I could see into the rooms above the other shops; some were lived in, others were not. Some were just stock rooms; a waiting room of things to be sold. Looking out at night, all along the street were shops with lit windows, others in darkness, some with their names illuminated for no one to see; the staff long gone home. Down below me I could see the heads of passers-by or the few cars driving single file.

Feeling safe in my secret hideout, protected from view by the height of my position, I felt like a spy. Outside the rattling sash window was a coil of barbed wire to keep off the pigeons. Seeming unimpressed by their displacement, they sat on the sills of the shops opposite, their jerky heads twitching as if joining me in listening for clues. At night I could watch people as if filming them without their knowledge; a man stops to light a cigarette in the shelter of a shop doorway, the same well-practised routine of striking the fizzing match and cradling the flame, then blowing it out with a puff through pursed lips, as he flings it into the gutter and strides on; a window shopping dog-walker is dragged along by its animal eager to get back to its bone; a stride of raucous men, just tumbled from the pub, looking for more fun, too early to go home; a couple of army lads in fatigues, in haste, as if they're on the run. And then they are gone. The street left in peace, except perhaps a throb of throaty engine noise from further up the hill. Stillness at last as the town makes its way home. Time for bed. Even the pigeons have gone.

Inside my room was my tidy little desk and pile of books, a Christmas xylophone, and tape recorder with microphone. My neat single bed with sheets and blankets that lay heavy on my feet, no duvet yet. David Cassidy looked across at Donny Osmond on the opposite wall. The one in deep unbuttoned denim shirt, the other, toothy grinned with perfect hair. The one leaning provocatively, head tilted back, coaxing the other to loosen up a bit.

Next door was Caroline's room, which also overlooked the street. She slipped into my life without irritation, her arrival a mere eighteen months after mine. Whenever we were introduced, as Lucinda and Caroline, it was like we came as a pair. As a child she had bright blonde hair and wide eyes that seemed to be trying to make sense of the world. Grandma used to call her 'My little apple'. I've always felt protective, yet admiring of her natural way of making people feel special. That is her gift. When she was born the midwife let out a sound as if she had been stung by a bee, and said, 'What's that on her face?' It was a small beauty mark in the shape of a diamond, perfectly delineated under her left eye. I always thought it beautiful. She's since had it removed.

Ma and Pa's room was next to ours at the rear. Sometimes you could hear Pa testing Ma on her mental arithmetic in bed.

You had to be nimble with your sums in the shop, especially since the first till we had didn't do addition. One night Ma woke to hear someone calling from downstairs. Nudging Pa awake, she sent him down to have a look. Descending the stairs in his nightshirt, a recent birthday present bought as a bit of fun and a change from his usual striped pyjamas, he made his way down into the darkened shop. The glare from a torch caught his attention as the officious voice behind it shone it directly into his face. It was a policeman who had found our door unlocked. Back then the policemen on nightshift checked each shop door one by one as they walked down the street on their beat, rattling each door in turn. When he came upon ours, he must have been surprised. We never left the shop door unlocked after that. The police used to come in for their sweets and tobacco and I am sure that the story of Pa in his nightshirt got round. It was just lucky that he hadn't been wearing the tasselled nightcap that had come as part of the set.

Out on the landing curved the low wooden bannisters with wooden balustrades. It was low even for me because the stairs were so steep. Lean over too far and you would be down in the stairwell in seconds. Sometimes we would have a night out with family, and be put to bed at our relatives' house when it got late. After driving us home, Pa would carry us up the steep flight of stairs to our rooms. Lifting us out of the car one by one, dozing in our nylon sleeping bags, the silky fabric tricky to grip. Heavy with sleep, I would think of feathers, believing that made me lighter.

The flat hadn't been lived in for some time by the previous incumbents. It was all a bit drab but fine for a while. The kitchen felt it wasn't quite on our side: the Belling cooker with its oven door difficult to close and the immersion heater that needed to think about it before letting hot water splutter out of its long narrow arm. The cupboards, too deep for my short arms, smelt of other people's shopping. Cutting the kitchen in two was a Formica counter like that in a fish and chip shop, but without the glass cabinets, or fish, and too high to be useful. At one end attached to a wall was a black and white Formica table and above it, hanging suspended, the drying rack.

The lounge next door was where we would head for, dumping satchels and school shoes in a pile, watching TV before homework. And here too, to enjoy Sunday lunches with grandparents arriving in their Sunday best, Grandma in her Crimplene dress and beads and hat, Grandpa in his three-piece suit, as we enjoyed roast lamb above the shop.

In the corner, the blue vinyl box record player spun the most eclectic mix of music you could possibly imagine; from Pinky and Perky to 'Rock Around the Clock', LPs, 45s and the odd 78s. The novelty song 'Hello Muddah, Hello Faddah' by Allan Sherman about a boy pleading to come home from summer camp, and Joyce Grenfell's deadpan monologue about nursery school children were our favourites. My parents had bought the player and all the records as a job lot, not long after they had got married. I liked it because it made me think of them at their most youthful, snuggled up together listening to Frank Sinatra's *Songs for Swingin' Lovers!* I remember one night when I couldn't sleep, when I was about four, coming downstairs to find them both in the early throes of decorating, stripping wallpaper as the record player kept them entertained. I joined in for a while, pulling strips off the wall in my pyjamas before being sent back to bed.

After living above the shop for a couple of years my mother's yearnings for the countryside became unbearable. She found a small cottage in Upwey, a village about four miles from Dorchester. It was liberating to have the freedom of the countryside after living above the shop. The cottage faced fields and at six o'clock you could see the cows coming home for milking. It was on the steepest hill I had ever seen, which played havoc with our games. If you dropped the ball playing catch, you had to charge so hard down the road to outrun it that it felt like your heels were up by your ears. The village had a wishing well where we used to go and throw in pennies for a wish.

It was while living here that I broke my wrist playing 'trapeze' on the farm gate at the top of Upwey Hill. From the age of about six, Caroline longed to join the circus. It wasn't the animals that excited her but the lure of swinging through the air like Gina Lollobrigida in the Hollywood blockbuster *Trapeze*. She had made up her mind and did not seem in the least fazed at the prospect of leaving us, her family, behind, and going off to live life on the high wire. She wrote letters to Billy's Smart Circus which she gave to Pa to post. The weeks went by and still she received no reply. Pa did his best to staunch her disappointment, saying it was probably difficult for the postman to find the letter box on a Big Top that was moving around the country all the time. She only found out years later that he had never sent them. It was a dilemma for him. I am not sure that that scenario is listed in any parenting manual, certainly none that I have ever seen.

Egged on by her, I slung my bent legs over the five bar gate and hung upside down. That was easy. The mistake was to take the act one step further and hang down vertically facing the gate with just my feet strained at a right-angle, hooked over the top bar. I dropped like a stone to the ground, landing hard on my right arm. I knew I had done something serious, as I heard the bone crack. I ran down the hill back to the cottage behind my crying sister, cradling my bendy, wobbling arm. We called Ma who was at the shop, and she screeched home in the Mini and drove me to hospital. My fractured radius was put in a plaster cast and I spent the next eight weeks learning to write with my left hand.

After we left the flat it transitioned from home to warehouse. The lounge became Pa's office, the dining table pushed up against the textured wallpaper, VAT notices and suppliers' phone numbers stuck to the wall. He kept a neat and orderly desk, accounts with figures encased in columns, tallied up and at hand. He was in tune with what we were spending, aware of what we could afford, like a pianist knowing the sound made by every single chord. My bedroom became filled with boxes where the bed had been; no ornaments or posters, no dressing gown hanging on the back of the door; no pile of books or fluffy slippers on the floor. I felt no sadness. Close the door and don't look back, that's what I had learned.

We had taken what we needed from the flat, we were moving on. It would not be home to anyone again, we were to be the last.

6

Stocking Up

I T WAS AN odd thing for a young teen to become expert in, but that is what I became – an expert in tobacco. We sold every brand there was, each one conjuring up its own marketing idyll. Golden Virginia with its sun-baked prairies, Player's Navy Cut for the sailors, and Clan in its tartan pouches for the hunting, shooting, fishing set. I liked the tins, which when you prised off the lid revealed little pleated paper skirts that kept the tobacco in place.

I learned that pipe tobacco came in ready rubbed or rough cut varieties and christened my teddy 'Bruno Rough Cut' after St Bruno tobacco. Bruno was a fuzzy-haired fellow and the name suited him perfectly, especially once I had taken the scissors to him and given his fur a bit of a choppy trim. We stocked a wide choice of pipe smokers' paraphernalia: aside from the pipes themselves there were pipe cleaners, flints, wicks, cans of lighter fuel and a whole array of tools for tamping down or scraping out tobacco. We always had a can of lighter fuel by the side of the till in case a customer wanted their lighter topped up on the spot.

Pa tried a pipe for a while. He felt that if he was selling

tobacco he should at least give it a go. He didn't get on with it, couldn't see what all the fuss was about. As he sucked and puffed and blew he complained that the blessed thing was out more than it was alight. It wasn't the habit for him. He took up marathon running instead.

It was fascinating to see the customers smoking roll-ups with orange or green Rizla papers. Some of them could even roll a cigarette with one hand as they paid for their tobacco with the other.

And as for cigarettes, we stocked the lot. The red and white packaging of Embassy No. 6, the navy blue of Rothmans, the purple streak of Silk Cut, and the cool minty green of Menthol Consulate. A carton of two hundred cigarettes, ten packets of twenty, were packaged together in a parcel, the outer wrapping different for each brand. Gold for Benson & Hedges, or B&H as everyone called them. We would unwrap them and stack them on the varnished wooden shelves, making sure to put the new stock underneath the current stock to keep it fresh. I can still see Mrs Eyres, one of our staff, engrossed in conversation with Pa as she unwrapped and stocked up the cigarettes.

How tactile is the little cardboard packet, designed to entice. Undo the thread to slide off its cellophane cover, like a snug fitting dress. Tip back the top of the pack as if supporting a head, preparing to kiss. Snatch off the gold foil slip from the smooth filter tips. And the smell, organic and fruity, good enough to eat, not to burn. These neat little boxes, a glamorous accessory hiding a morbid intention. The bubbly, putrid lungs that I would later nurse bore no relation to the perfect symmetry of these charming little packs. The gasps for breath, the wheezing effort, the heaving sack of bones. The smoker hunched, straining every thoracic muscle to open the chest and breathe in nicotine-free air.

Even before I had been a nurse, selling tobacco didn't make me want to smoke. Chain-smoking customers with nicotine-stained fingers and a fag stuck to their lower lip weren't a great advertisement for the habit. Anyway, it was too expensive. When crisps were 3½p a packet, twenty cigarettes would set you back 50p. But I did like the accoutrements of smoking; metal cigarette cases that snapped shut in your hand and lighters that lit with the flick of a thumb.

Some of the stock that we had inherited from the previous owners didn't sell well. In fact, I don't think we sold any of it. Sobranie, the long Russian cocktail cigarettes in bright pastel pink and purple, yellow and green with metallic foil filters, sat forlorn on the shelf. The black Bakelite cigarette holders studded with diamanté, fine and elegant, Marlene Dietrich-style, languished in the window undesired. I don't know the woman that these were intended for, I never met her. My hunch was that it was Mrs Walker herself, from whom we bought the shop. I imagined her reclining of an evening in her negligée with a glass of vodka, lighting up a Sobranie in a cigarette holder, making believe she was Russian royalty in her winter palace.

I never saw Pa smoke a cigarette. A pint of beer and a handful of peanuts were more his passion. He had toyed with the idea of running a pub once. He liked the idea of sharing half a shandy with the regulars as they entertained each other with their stories. He gave up the idea as too much of a commitment, and anyway, he couldn't get Ma on board with that one. No doubt she would have pulled pints and served snacks, but it wouldn't have given her the necessary satisfaction and outlet for her creativity. With a pub they would have been tied to a particular brewery with regulations and missives from on high. My parents needed creative freedom, to make something of their own and do it their way. They weren't to be constrained by rules.

And that's why they were good fun to work with. 'Would you like to stock up the bars, Lucinda?' Pa would say, tearing off a paper bag and handing it to me with the pen from behind his ear to make my list. It was a fun job, seeing which chocolate bars needed filling up and working out how many to bring up from the cellar below. The calculation had to be exact. If you tried to pile too many bars on top of each other, they would slide off the sloped display and cover up the bar below. Once I had made my list, I would go down to the cellar and search for the boxes containing the bars I was after.

The cellar was accessed by a narrow set of wooden stairs off a short passageway at the back of the shop. There was a little wooden gate that we used to swing across the top of the stairs if ever there were customers browsing boxes of chocolates that were displayed there. If anyone had stepped back too far into the stairwell, they would have had a horrible fall.

The cellar was quite big because it ran beneath the entire width of the premises, underneath both our sweet shop and the greengrocers. At the bottom of the cellar stairs on the left were two rooms. The one underneath the back of the shop had probably once been an office. In one corner against the wall was a broad wooden desk, and on the floor a large cast iron safe. It had a heavy blacked door, stiff from disuse. The safe was always left ajar, Pa preferring instead to use a hiding hole he had fashioned under the floorboards in the flat upstairs. In front of the desk was an old swivel chair, its red vinyl seat cracked and indented with wear. Who had sat here? Judging by the width of the indentation, someone with a larger rear than most, who didn't value sunlight. Pa always used the office in our lounge. None of us ever sat here.

The cellar room at the front was the main storage area for the stock. It wasn't decorous, it was functional; it only needed to be clean and dry as per the instructions on the wrappers and packets. The sweets and tobacco were stored in old orange boxes piled one on top of the other, wooden crates of rough-hewn slats once laden with apples and lettuces on sale in the shop above. Their faded and torn pictures remained, photos of tropical fruit bidding the buyer to 'Enjoy Fyffes bananas!' Homemade shelving, improvised, from the make do and mend generation. From the look of them, they had been there a long time. Here boxes were piled high with chocolate bars, tobacco and weigh-out sweets, their bright 'eat-me' packaging subdued in the cool, dim cellar.

The cellar was the ideal place to store the stock. It kept the sweets and tobacco in a state of suspended animation until it was sold. Keeping everything at a constant temperature was important to maintain its freshness and value. If chocolate is kept in fluctuating temperatures it can develop chocolate bloom, where it takes on a dullness and loses its shine. It is still edible but it doesn't look very appealing.

Immediately ahead of you at the bottom of the stairs was what had once been the coal bunker, with the coal hole above on the street. I found it quite a romantic notion to think of a horse-drawn cart stopping outside the shop and a bag of coal being poured into the chute to feed the coal-fired bread ovens below. Now it was just a place where we stored the rubbish. We had to collapse all the cartons or we would have been swimming in boxes, Pa even taking to climbing into the full bins and jumping on top of them to squash them down further. Then he would have to lug the heavy metal dustbins up the cellar stairs to put them out in the street for collection.

We were happy when the street later became pedestrianised as this part of the cellar extended underneath the road, and Pa was always worried that one of the heavy lorries that used to park outside to deliver our stock might one day plunge down into the cellar below. His engineering eyes were alert to the fact that the cellar had been built to specifications to accommodate a lighter road tonnage.

The room to the right of the stairs was where the bread ovens were. They weren't visible, but we all knew they were there, like a landmark commemorating an historic event, a reminder of what had happened here before our time. We used this part of the cellar for any seasonal stock, so most of the time it lay empty. But at Easter time it was teeming with chocolate eggs.

Standing in the cellar, you could hear the comforting creak of floorboards above; footfall familiar and unseen, the distant ring of the bell and the muffled voices of customers. It smelt of cardboard and faintly of chocolate and tobacco; a nice smell, the cool air chilling your nostrils, like breathing in menthol. During the heatwave of 1976, the worst drought for a hundred years, it felt wonderful to retreat here to its coolness.

It felt cavernous, the black matte concrete floor and the dark ceiling blurring the edges of its perimeters; an amorphous space, illuminated by a bare bulb. Whatever the season, the weather, day or night, it was always the same in here. In this subterranean hollow where the seasons had no influence and natural light was kept at bay, like the stacks of stock around you, you became suspended in time.

7

Money

Until we had the shop, I had never really seen money, except for the few coins that were pressed into my hand by a grandparent or aunt with the whisper, 'Buy yourself an ice cream.' Once we had the shop, cash was on daily view.

Sometimes my sister and I would help with the cashing up. This involved tipping the day's takings onto the dining room table, piling up the coins into one pound stacks, and sorting the notes into bundles of fifty or one hundred pounds each. Sometimes we would come across a fifty pound note, its importance highlighted by its bright red colour. We would normally only have the one, which made it all the more special. Holding it in my hand was like holding Willy Wonka's Golden Ticket. Just think of the fun you could have with that.

We liked the pictures on the back of the notes: the Duke of Wellington, William Shakespeare and Florence Nightingale with her radiant lamp. The sensation of holding a wad of notes in your hand, the slightly grainy texture and dusty papery smell, was like no other. Old notes felt grubby, aged and frayed. Sometimes we would need to give them first aid, gently mending the tears with Sellotape. If you could follow the fingerprint trail and see where the money had been, what a fascinating journey that would be. But I liked the new notes best, the ones that hadn't yet been through a thousand hands, folded and squashed into wallets, purses and back pockets.

We would sort the notes into their own family piles, the pound notes, the tens and twenties, making sure the Queen's head faced up the same way. I still like to keep the notes in my wallet like that. The lone fifty would sit on its own. We would hold the notes up to the light to see the watermark, strangely beautiful, a work of art in hiding. It was special, it had to be, with the Queen's head on it and the official sounding words. We would study the inscription, 'I promise to pay the bearer on demand the sum of five pounds', and the rather scrawly signature of the Chief Cashier. You would have thought they could have picked someone with neater handwriting to write on a pound note.

Looking at the money, Pa would say, 'That's a lot of wine gums!' and he was right. That pile of cash on our dining table was the return on seeing my parents stand up all day in our shop, serving customers, weighing out sweets or selling tobacco. If they had been farmers or gardeners, this would have been their harvest. We all joined in with the gathering of it, getting it to where it needed to go, into the bank.

After the money was counted, Pa would put it all into a zip-up bank deposit bag. He would take it to the night safe at the bank two doors along. There was no security firm or heavy mob, just Pa with a pouch of cash hidden under a newspaper. Turning the key to the wall safe, and pulling open the drawer, he would let the day's takings drop to safety below. We never had any trouble and this must have been the practice for many traders in the town.

Once he had deposited the cash, he would replenish the till with the float. This meant filling the coin compartments with the same amount of coins each day so that we would know how much money was in the till at the start of trading. Deducting this sum would enable us to calculate the day's takings. Once he had made up the float for the following day, he would place it in a gap underneath the floorboards in the lounge for safe keeping.

The float was made up of the minimum of cash that we needed to carry to be able to serve the initial customers of the day. Occasionally, we would be left short of change when a string of customers might try to pay for a penny box of matches or ten Benson & Hedges, costing twenty-five pence, with a five pound note. If so, one of us would pop into the bank or to Stuart Turner, the tobacconist across the street, to get some change.

If we were having a particularly busy day, Pa would collect up a wad of notes and take them upstairs to hide under the floorboards for safe keeping before adding them to the total for cashing up at the end of the trading day. Overnight we would remove the money tray with its compartments for coins and spring-loaded levers to keep the notes in place, and leave the till drawer open without any cash in it so that if the shop was broken into, the till wouldn't be damaged by the drawer being forced open. In the morning, when we opened up, we would slide the money tray containing the float into the till drawer to start a new day of trading.

When it came to money Ma would say, 'Don't tell everyone your business. Don't tell people how much we've taken today.' People only see the car or the house, they don't see how much you might be in hock at the bank, the overdrafts, the bank loans, the financial arrangements. And turnover is not profit. People don't know your overheads, the expenses that need to be paid. You might be at private school or buying a new car, but people can't see the delicate balance that is going on behind the scenes between the business, the bank and the customer.

Once I started working in the shop on Saturdays, Pa would

pay me wages like the rest of the staff, in cash, in a brown payslip envelope. Opening it up to find pound notes inside that I had earned was a real treat. Pocket money is one thing, but earning your own cash is a different thing altogether. Pocket money was a gift to me as a child, wages were recognition of my value as a worker. 'Happiness is not in the mere possession of money; it lies in the joy of achievement, in the thrill of creative effort,' said Franklin D. Roosevelt. He got that right. Holding the crisp notes and shiny coins (I'm sure Pa picked out the newest ones to give to me) was happiness indeed.

Money is like a passport, it guarantees your free passage. You have the Queen's protection. Money gives freedom to do and buy what you want, to feel in control in your life. It gives you the power of choice. Money is noble, it is what it is. It is how you earn and spend it that alters its complexion.

And so I had a healthy relationship with money. It wasn't until I went to school and was taught by nuns that I realised there was a more widely held view about money, based on fear. They taught me that having or aspiring to have money is not a good thing. We were taught that money was inevitably linked to misery. I used to think it odd. Money was neutral in my eyes, and to teach us that money should be shunned didn't sit well, bearing in mind that ours was a fee paying school and that our parents worked hard and made personal sacrifices to send us there. What of the power of money to do good, to change people's lives for the better?

But a relationship with money can also be a fraught one. After a year of running the sweet shop, Pa realised that he had made a mistake. The shop wasn't going to work. He had studied the accounts and knew that it wasn't viable. He and Ma were working all hours, evenings and Sundays. They couldn't squeeze any more income out of the business if they tried. They had kept their overheads low, not employing staff, and living above the shop, but it wasn't enough.

One of the difficulties they faced was that they had started out in debt. While the proceeds from the sale of Tiffany's guest house had secured the shop lease (we hadn't bought the freehold), they had to borrow money to buy the stock. In fact it had been an oversight of the previous owners. They had agreed on a figure for the sale of the lease, but just as the deal was being done, the owners said that they had forgotten to add the cost of the stock. Ma and Pa had sunk every penny they had into buying the lease and had nothing left, so the owners offered to lend them the money to complete the sale for the stock. So they started off with a debt to the previous owners, a sum that needed to be repaid each month. This pushed them into the red. As it turned out, the stock wasn't worth the value they had paid, as much of it was rotten. Dried-out tobacco and stale sweets had to be thrown away.

One night after closing, Pa walked out of the shop and didn't come back. Ma was really worried. She phoned my grandfather Wilson who lived in the town, who went out looking for him. He drove around the streets and checked the pubs but couldn't find him anywhere. Pa returned at around midnight. He had been sitting in the park in the dark, looking for an answer. 'I just don't see how to make this work, Jude,' he said to my mother, 'the shop isn't big enough.'

8

Staying Afloat

A s is often the case in my experience, things tend to turn up. Opportunities can arise where you least expect. By chance, the Walkers' son Ron, who ran the greengrocers next door, came to Pa to say he was thinking of selling up and to ask whether my father would be interested in taking on the lease. He had had enough of the fruit and veg trade and fancied moving to the South of France to open an ice cream parlour.

Ah, now for the fun! How to make this work. What to do with an extra shop? After much deliberating, they decided that a larger sweet shop wasn't the answer. Ma came up with the idea of a card and gift shop, which was a natural pairing with a sweet shop. I remember a family outing to Bournemouth, traipsing around card shops with a rep, doing 'market research', or spying as Caroline and I called it. We would go round the shops, looking at the type of stock they carried and see how busy they were. 'Now we're just going to look as if we're buying a card, you two,' Ma would say to us, as we stepped into the role of undercover agents acting on behalf of our family enterprise.

After borrowing money against the business, the deal was done, and we took on the premises next door. The signage

Osmond's at 51 South Street, Dorchester.

above the shop was changed to read *Osmond's Tobacconist & Confectioner, Cards & Gifts* in a broad banner reaching across both premises, the two shops being united once more.

We all worked together clearing the wooden crates that had displayed cabbages and cauliflowers, getting the shop ready for its transformation. Pa painted it throughout, and took down the wall that had divided the grocers and a store room at the back to enlarge the shop. Card stands arrived, display units with little tiered sections at the top and drawers below. The stock was limited at first, but it was a start: birthday cards, cuddly toys and small gifts.

It felt like we were on to something, a bigger, better, new beginning. The day we opened was an understated affair. There was no stampede, no grand opening with balloons and Champagne. We stood by the display table, Pa on my right, Ma and Caroline on my left. Our first customer was a grandmother who bought a teddy for her grandson. I put it into one of the larger white paper bags that was more used to wrapping boxes of *Milk Tray* and made our first sale. Osmond's Tobacconist & Confectioner, Cards & Gifts was up and running.

The card shop retained its original frontage, which was the same as the sweet shop with a glazed wooden door with diagonal brass bar handle, flanked either side by two wooden framed windows. Now that we had the other shop we had two more shop windows to dress. Ma relished the opportunity to be creative. Sunday walks were spent collecting props, such as interesting-shaped branches or fir cones that she could use in her window display. Using a long twisted willow branch that we had collected from a walk in Puddletown Woods, she once created a woodland scene for an array of furry rabbits and chicks.

Customers loved the countryside. We could sell anything with a bird or a badger on it. If Ma did a themed window with tasselled catkins or pussy willow, customers flocked in. We had a cuckoo clock; children would sit on the floor and wait for it to chime while their mum went to buy a card.

The card and gift shop became Ma's domain. She worked there while Pa ran the sweet shop next door. Ma knew her clientele. That first year of running the sweet shop had in effect been her market research. She knew the locals, the farmers, the people from the villages who only came into Dorchester on market day. She knew the people in the town, the other shopkeepers and hoteliers, and the holidaymakers who would return year after year. Just like the bed and breakfast guests, she was aware of what they wanted, what would make their holiday special. She knew her market and their budget. She stocked the shop with all of them in mind.

We had Alresford teddies, and dolls in handmade dresses for the grandparents and parents to buy; silk scarves, velour nightdress cases and satin evening bags for the husbands to give to their wives; Peanuts stationery and Wade Whimsy animal figures, which were small and inexpensive enough to be bought with pocket money, or as a holiday treat for the children. A postcard stand arrived, its twirling metal frame chained to the wall in front of the shop to stop it sliding down the slightly sloped pavement on its castors or being wheeled off by some joy-riding youth. We stocked it up with Salmon's seaside and town views of Weymouth Bay and Bowleaze Cove, Dorchester's Borough Gardens and the poet and novelist Thomas Hardy's birthplace. It attracted the tourists and the French exchange students, who might also buy a box of souvenir fudge to take back home.

With time we had cards for every occasion and celebration, from new home to new baby, from 'with love', to 'with sympathy'. Ma handpicked every card, every gift tag, every sheet of wrapping paper. She had commercial sense, perhaps learned from her father's talk at the dinner table about his job as a manager of a string of butchers' shops. She chose carefully, selecting only what she thought her customers liked. 'If I like what I'm selling, I can be enthusiastic,' she would say.

Judith Osmond, Ma, amongst the cards.

Being part of a family business gave us a sense of unity, which was even closer than just being a family. Being known in the town gave us a kind of pass, being 'tarred with the same brush', but in a good way. It gave us a cloak of invincibility, together we were stronger. 'We are the Osmonds' became a family mantra that Ma would declare when she felt the slightest pang of injustice, sometimes tongue in cheek. 'We're not having that, we're the Osmonds,' she would say. It wasn't based on arrogance, just a bit of healthy family pride.

As the business expanded, and as we got on our feet, we needed to take on staff. Over the years we had a lovely mix of people who worked for us. There was a girl called Janet who was probably in her late teens. She was tall and lean with long dark hair and used to wear chocolate brown cords with cowboy boots, and shirts with a bohemian frill down the front. She felt like a romantic, nomadic spirit, smoking roll-ups and spending her spare time at music festivals. She was very easy company and used to work with me in the summer holidays. I enjoyed her sense of humour, particularly the way we would have fun together over some of the more eccentric characters who used to come in the shop. One such, who we named The Druid, swanned in to buy half a pound of wine gums every week wearing a full length cape and hood up over his head. I think it was a he, we barely saw his face, and he hardly uttered a word, pointing at the sweets and handing over the exact money in change. I always felt that working for us was an interlude for Janet, to take a breath before setting off on an adventure. After several years with us, she left and moved away.

There was also Mrs Eyres, a quietly conscientious woman in her fifties. She wasn't known by her first name, Bertha, probably because she was older than the other people who worked for us. Before joining us she had worked in a shoe shop in the town, which she didn't like much, so was very pleased when she heard there was a job going in the sweet shop.

Julie was twenty-two years old when she started working for us. She had previously worked in the stockings department of Houghton's, a small family-run department store in Dorchester. Ma used to walk through the store on her way to the car park and see Julie standing behind her counter. She had made such a good impression on Ma that when Julie came for interview for our newly opened card shop, Ma gave her the job on the spot. It was a good decision. Julie was a very hard worker, keen to learn and a joy to have around. She worked for us for fifteen years.

Of all the staff, Julie was closest to us in age, being just seven years older than me; she was like the big sister I didn't have. Any questions that either Caroline or I had about boys, make-up or teenage angst that weren't answered in my *Jackie* magazines were dealt with in confidence by Julie. We felt lucky to have her on our side.

Julie was sensible and stylish, alert and current. Caroline and I adored her fashion sense, her soft permed curls and platform boots, her corduroy A-line skirts and V-neck sweaters in fawns and beige, russet and browns. I don't think she ever wore the same outfit twice. We admired her skill at make-up, her soft blue eyeshadow and tawny lips and perfectly painted nails in shades of plum. Julie was polished, punctual and polite.

She earned seventeen pounds per week working full time. Everyone received their wages at the end of the week in a brown envelope, but if we had had a good day, Pa would add a little extra to their pay packet.

'Here you are, I've put a little extra in for you. Thank you for your help today,' Pa would say.

In 1979 there was a promotion in the town to find the shop assistant of the year. Julie saw this as a great opportunity and enthusiastically encouraged family and customers to sign her voting form. It was so exciting the day she won. The Lady Mayor and Town Crier came to have a photograph taken with

Julie Plummer, formerly Lacey, receiving her prize as
Dorchester Shop Assistant of the Year 1979, from the Lady Mayor
Beth Boothman, heralded by the Town Crier.

Julie's prize-giving outside Osmond's with Caroline,
the Town Crier, Lady Mayor Beth Boothman,
Julie, Clive and Judith Osmond, 1979.

her in our shop. The *Dorset Echo* printed the announcement and the photograph of a proud Julie holding her prize of a gilt silver cup and bouquet of flowers.

In the card shop we were also lucky to have Irene, who, as Ma was always at pains to point out, was married to a police officer. This suggested a serious and reserved air, and made me uncertain of how to treat her. But it was all bravado on Ma's part and Irene would shrug off the label as if she couldn't quite believe it either. I have heard other people say that the greatest strain in running a business is finding and keeping good staff. We were very lucky on that score. We had some very special people working with us.

9

Saturday Girl

FROM ABOUT THE age of thirteen I took on a Saturday and holiday job in the sweet shop with Pa. From an earlier age I had been able to step in and serve customers if we were busy or if Pa needed to nip down to the cellar for stock. By the time of my early teens we were living in a house in Dorchester and Pa and I would drive in together, to open up for a quarter to nine. Unlocking the door, we would go into the narrow shop, Pa flicking on the lights as he went, then popping upstairs to collect the cash tray to put into the till ready for the day's trading.

With the shop established and doing well, Pa bought himself a brand new Lancia. He'd always sworn he would never buy a new car. It was madness, he used to say, it depreciated in value the moment you drove it off the forecourt. But with the Lancia, he succumbed. I loved it too, the sleek metallic gold bodywork, the plush velour upholstery and that beautiful smell you only get with new cars, very different from the lingering aroma of tobacco and body odour that permeates used ones. It was much better than the Renault 16s we used to have. We had a whole fleet of those over the years. Their suspension was a bit flabby in comparison, rolling you to one side as you went

Lucinda weighing out Mint Imperials.

round corners, like on a fairground ride. The Lancia HPE hugged you as it gripped the road. Sadly, it did not live up to its promise, requiring two replacement engines and three new gear boxes. Even then it wasn't right. The ignition was temperamental, taking several attempts to get the thing going.

South Street had a particularly tenacious traffic warden at this time who enforced the strict 'loading only' restriction very diligently. Pa would take his chances, parking outside the shop for a few minutes while we opened up, often leaving the engine running in case he needed to make a quick getaway.

The traffic warden could soon be relied upon to turn up just at the wrong moment. On receiving an alert from a watchful customer, Pa would dash out to the car and make a timely escape to the safety of the car park. The manager of Curry's, Paul, used to do the same thing. He had an open top MGB Roadster that he used to park outside the store. On seeing Pa make a dash for it, he would come striding out from behind the washing machines and take a running jump into the MG. He was so tall that he didn't need to open the car door, he just leapt in over the top, and sped off, his head and shoulders sitting proud above the windscreen. A quarter of an hour later, Pa and Paul would be walking up South Street together, looking like a couple of schoolboys who had just got one over the teacher.

When we opened up, South Street was generally still quiet except for an early morning shopper or sales assistant heading into work. One of my first jobs was to drag the revolving postcard stand to its spot outside on the pavement. It was a tricky task requiring me to bend low and grab its splayed castored legs, which, like a shopping trolley, wanted to take it in all different directions. Getting it down the step was the challenge, steadying it to stop it nose-diving and scattering hundreds of postcards all over the street. Picking up all those was a job I wouldn't have fancied.

Standing up I would look down the street, catching the eye of early shoppers on a mission. Looking left towards the Corn Exchange, I could see the father and son on the barrows, piling up mounds of reddish nectarines or green apples, the heavy metal scales poised ready to weigh out pounds of fruit and veg, the strung wad of brown paper bags blowing like petticoats in the breeze.

I would serve any customers in the card shop until Julie arrived at 9am to take over. She would arrive cheerful as always with perfect hair and make-up, wearing yet another outfit that I had never seen before.

Lunchtime trade brought the shop workers popping in during breaks; the lads from Curry's across the road coming for their Golden Wonder crisps and cans of Fanta to accompany their homemade sandwich; the manager of Frisby's shoe shop for his single cigar. He came in to buy one every day, explaining that if he bought an entire packet he would have to smoke the lot.

I enjoyed working with Pa and learning new skills such as how to weigh out a quarter pound of sweets. Pa taught me how to tear off a white paper bag from the loop of string on which they hung and spread my other hand into the bag so that it stood open. Then I would pick up the little metal scoop and plunge it into the sweets, letting them roll off the scoop into the bag on the scales, checking the weight as I went. I would fill the bag with sweets to four ounces for a quarter pound or eight ounces for a half pound. He taught me how to finish off by swinging the bag by its corners, looping it over so that the bag sealed itself. I got quite quick at it. The scoop made different sounds depending on the types of sweets. If it was something hard and crisp like liquorice torpedoes, it would sound like walking on pebbles; with something soft like coconut mushrooms, there would be no sound at all.

Putting the jars back on the shelf after weighing out the sweets had its own technique. There were some lightweight plastic jars that were easy to handle, but most of them were glass and heavy enough when they were empty let alone filled to the brim. You had to hold the jar close to your chest with both hands then put the heel of one hand underneath its glass bottom and push it skywards in one quick movement, extending your arm above you, like the Statue of Liberty. Then you would need to nudge it onto the shelf above your head with your fingers.

This was an action we would repeat many times in a day. If I was struggling, Pa would appear and push the jar up out of my hand onto the shelf for me. It was definitely easier if you were taller. If you felt you weren't going to make it, you had to be ready to take a step back and catch the jar as it started to fall.

Most of the empty jars were sent back with the reps, but we did have requests for empty jars from some of the customers. One woman liked to use them for storing her balls of knitting wool and several others said they were ideal for pickling onions.

We didn't have a till that calculated the change so you either did the sums in your head or on the back of a paper bag. If the customer was paying with notes, we would insert them into the metal clip on the front of the till so that we would remember how much change to give, counting it out into the customer's hand.

Although skills can of course be learned, it soon became clear that Pa didn't quite have Ma's expert eye when it came to buying stock for the card and gift shop. Most of the time Ma did the buying, but sometimes a stray rep would arrive unannounced on a day when Ma wasn't working. Ma only found out what Pa had ordered when it arrived.

'Clive, what have you bought now?' Ma would say as she unwrapped the unfamiliar items. 'Customers don't want gravy boats! How many did you buy?'

'Only twenty.'

'Oh no.'

'He was such a nice bloke, and I don't think he had sold much,' Pa would reply.

This was not what Ma wanted to sell at all. She was after crafted goods, made by hand or in small workshops, things that customers wouldn't have seen elsewhere. There were other shops in the town where customers could buy kitchenware.

Fortunately, though, these items were easily disposed of on the 'sale table', otherwise known as 'Pa's bad buys'. This was a small round wicker table that Ma would set up from time to time to clear the unwanted stock. Alternatively, 'Pa's bad buys' got given away as donations. 'You'll have a gravy boat in a minute!' Julie would say to the person who had come in looking for a raffle prize. Pa would return from the upstairs stockroom, formerly our lounge, bearing a stainless steel gravy boat complete with box.

'There you go, sir! Good luck with your fundraising,' Pa would say handing over the offering to the bemused raffle collector, who had probably anticipated receiving a box of chocolates. Julie and Ma would smile at each other, relieved to be shot of another one.

When Caroline was old enough she started working in the card shop on Saturdays alongside Julie. As an encouragement for Caroline learning how to use the till, Pa promised her a penny for every customer she served that day. Julie let Caroline serve them all, so by the end of the day Pa had quite a payout.

There was never a bad atmosphere in the shop, Ma and Pa's personalities setting the tone and feel of the place. They enjoyed being around people. Pa wasn't the sort of boss who would sit out the back with his nose in the sports page, or be stuck to the chair in his office. He enjoyed what he did, and meeting people was part of the fun.

He was always on the go, working with him was easy. For the most part I served customers, weighing out sweets and taking the money. Sometimes Pa would find me other jobs to do, but none that he wouldn't do himself. He was a dab hand with the broom, whisking it out from behind the till and deftly sweeping up dropped sweets or pools of powdered sugar. He could do it so quickly that, even with a customer on the threshold, he would have whipped out the soft bristled brush and danced it round the shop before the advancing customer had even noticed.

Sometimes Pa would ask me to hold the fort while he nipped down the road to run a short errand. Pa knew everyone in the town. A five minute dash might turn into a half hour delay with him stopping to chat to customers or fellow traders along the way. He rarely returned empty handed, unable to resist the fresh-out-the-oven iced buns or just-arrived cherries off the barrows. His unexpected treats made our tea breaks special. We looked forward to what he might come back with next, hoping for something sweet to eat while poring over the photo stories in *Jackie*.

Pa had mastered his working uniform, the clothes of choice for working in the shop. In the winter he would wear trousers with a navy blue Guernsey sweater, bought during our camping holidays to Cornwall. It smelt of oiled wool and was ideal for a place of work where the door to the street was continuously being opened and closed. In the summer he swapped the sweater for a short sleeved shirt. He was a stylish man, keeping his beard neatly trimmed and unruly locks of hair flattened with a dampened comb. Some days he would still be walking around with the comb in his head at lunchtime. If you wanted a pencil, you need look no further than the top of his right ear. You knew if he needed to remember something because it would be written on a square of masking tape covering the face of his watch. He kept his and our shoes perfectly polished as part of his Sunday evening ritual. Looking down along the line of standing feet at school assembly, you could work out which shoes were yours by the gleam.

As closing time loomed Julie would get out the old vacuum cleaner, pre-Dyson, which probably blew out more dust than it sucked, wheezing and straining like an old chain-smoker. It was a sign that we were shutting soon, a sign for customers not to start coming in unless they were quick and for those just killing time before their bus to look for another temporary refuge. We now closed our shop at 5.30 on the dot every night, or at least that was the aim. After being on your feet all day, when closing time comes, you just want to lock up and head home.

'Right, that's it, Lucinda. It's five-thirty, put "closed" on the door,' Pa would say. We used to have an open and closed sign on the door of the sweet shop. Slide the little plastic lever one way and the sign said open, shift it the other and the message read, 'Sorry we are closed'. Originally it had been a picture promoting a brand of cigarettes. 'We are open for Rothmans,' the caption read, but Ma didn't like it. Pa replaced it with an anniversary card he had given her one year. Now it was Constable's *Hay Wain* that greeted customers.

Then with a flick of the lights we would leave the shop in darkness, locking up the treats for another day.

10

A Shop For All Seasons

I N THE SUMMER there was a natural ebb and flow of people strolling up and down the street outside, like a river with its tributaries constantly trickling. As the morning progressed there would be a rising tide of people, as the call of the town lured them out of their homes ahead of the threat of Sunday closing. Customers were relaxed, looking ahead to holidays planned or talking of holidays had. The Convent girl boarders in boaters, blazer sleeves coolly pushed up their wrists, counted down the days until school was out.

We left the door open to let in any breeze, otherwise the shop became a hothouse. Even so, the summer sun warmed the sweets, intensifying their stickiness and releasing their flavours into the shop. Serving sweets in the summer became more of a treat; just the act of removing the lid of a jar of clotted cream toffees released a warm caramel aroma to savour. Sometimes, the boiled fruit sweets would stick to the inside of the jar and you would have to chip at them with the metal scoop, firing sugary shards around the glass.

In the summer, with the door open, we would feel part of the street, able to see customers coming to us before they had arrived. Our shop felt so much bigger than it did in the winter, like a house does with its windows and doors thrown open to the air. If we were quiet, I might pop upstairs to look for stock, to top up the postcards perhaps. The sash windows would be open to the noises of the street, the sound of feet on the pavement, chatter and banter from below. I could hear the bell from the door downstairs and the thumping shut of the till. Then sometimes Pa would summon me back, and I would descend to find the shop suddenly packed, with Pa amidst a sea of customers, as I did a quick scan to see who to serve next.

When the schools broke up, summer began in earnest. The school kids took their place in the town, confident and noisy, shopping in gangs. People seemed freer, as if discarding their winter clothes had given them a lightness of mind. People even smelt different, of clothes dried outside, and the floating aroma of suntan oil, Hawaiian Tropic or Ambre Solaire. Shoppers in sunglasses planned trips to the beach. People came out of their shells and into the light with a seasonal body consciousness, revealing bare white skin or newly bronzed limbs.

Older women in pastel-coloured chiffon scarves protecting just-permed hair, the younger ones with exposed painted toenails. The garments of fun, shorts and sun dresses, sandals and flip-flops. Even the older women in their heavy corsetry revealed their knees and upper arms. In summer they would shed their winter hats and stockings for lighter versions, a routine mirrored in their homes, replacing winter curtains with lightweight summer ones.

And then there was Wimbledon to look forward to when the shop was pervaded with the gentlemanly commentary of Dan Maskell as we snatched sips of Pa's homemade Coke floats in between serving customers. Sometimes as the matches got tense, we would have a huddle of customers around the radio, listening to the reverberating rallies of Borg, McEnroe or Connors, as they battled it out for tennis's greatest prize. I, like Pa, cheered on mild-mannered Borg. How we longed to champion a Brit.

We did have a few losses. For a while we had an open chest freezer out of which we sold ice creams in the summer. Due to the demand for ice cold drinks we stocked up the freezer with cans of Coke to chill them down for an hour or two. Some got left in the freezer overnight, and when we found them the next day, they had exploded, leaking solidified froth over the Lyons Maid ice cream.

We didn't have unsightly fly tape like they had in the butchers. Pa took command of a fly swatter that would coax away any inclined wasp and, with a flick of his wrist, send it plummeting to the floor and out of the door.

For lunch breaks I would grab my handbag and step out into the sunny street, joining the coursing stream of people, an intertwining thoroughfare of shoppers on the move. Some days I might head up to the market. The separate pitches, the diverse mix: records and engine parts, Adam Ant badges and jewellery pots, Grandad collar shirts and car cleaning kits. Walk on further and you would see something different again.

The films at the cinema were about summer loving and disco dancing, about having fun. South Walks became resplendent in horse chestnut leaves, creating an ornamental walkway that felt special, as if the town had cause for celebration.

And the carnival and circus arrived, heralding to everyone that it was all right to have a good time. The carnival parade passed in front of our shop. We used to invite Grandma to sit at the lounge window, looking out onto the street, with the huge sash window thrown open to give her the best view. As time approached for the procession to start, the pavements would slowly fill up. There were no metal barriers to hold people back, people just stood where they pleased. The procession of decked-out lorries would start in the market near the brewery. Gradually you would be able to hear the melodic notes from the

St John Ambulance brass band interspersed with the piercing peeps from the steam engine leading the way. The lorries would drive past slowly, giving you just enough time to work out if you could recognise anyone, and throw a few pennies into the rattled buckets of the pageant performers. It wasn't the Mardi Gras, it was very homemade, but it was a draw nonetheless, created and put on by the town.

One year our Girl Guides pack had our own float, a seed merchant's lorry decked out with the tableau of an anti-slavery theme. I got away lightly, playing the part of a plantation owner. Caroline didn't fare so well. She was coated head to foot in some sort of black tar. It turned out to be semi-permanent and she, like the rest of the pack who represented slaves, walked around for several days with a tidemark of blackened skin. I still remember the ripple of horror when she and Ma found out that the stain didn't wash off, scrubbing her skin in the bath till it was sore.

To celebrate Dorchester Carnival, there was a competition for the best themed shop window. Ma and Julie created an animal pageant with a display of soft toys complete with handmade cardboard cart and a signpost saying, 'This way to the carnival!' George's the butchers kindly donated a piece of artificial grass, which helped set the rural scene. But Ma and Julie didn't have long to admire their handiwork. Almost as soon as they had finished someone came in and bought the stuffed donkey that was pulling the cart, and the next customer bought all twelve of the toy rabbits that were sitting in the cart, one for each of her nephews and nieces.

'Isn't it amazing, Julie? We've had that donkey two years and it has never sold. Put it in the window and it's gone within minutes!'

By the time the judging took place, all that was left in the window was the empty cart and the sign.

Around the time of the Queen's Silver Jubilee, in 1977,

and later, the wedding of Charles and Diana, we stocked a small selection of royal souvenirs. Ma was cautious despite the reps' rapturous enthusiasm. 'Oh Mrs Osmond, you'll need hundreds. They'll sell like hotcakes!' the reps would say. She remained unconvinced, which was fortunate, as we sold very few. People were interested to look, but not necessarily to buy a commemorative plate of Charles and Di. We did, however, sell a lot of rosettes, in a combination of red, white and blue. People bought them to wear at street parties or adorn homemade hats. We made them on a manual bow-maker machine that was heavy and cumbersome. It involved turning a metal handle round and round as you watched the satin-ribboned rosette take shape. Using it was a novelty at first, but by the time you had made about ten rosettes, the fun had worn off. We could barely keep up with demand, taking it in shifts to make a dozen or two at a time. When we ran low there was a sense of foreboding as we said to each other, 'I know what I'll be doing at lunchtime.'

A circus tent used to be pitched every summer near Lodmoor Hill in Weymouth. It would arrive for a week and then be gone. Although there were no circus parades through the town, no brass brand or elephants as in *Trapeze*, a couple of friendly performers stopped by our shop with a wad of printed posters looking to advertise the show. But they were entertaining in themselves. The Ringmaster came in wearing his top hat and tails, his exaggerated courteous mannerisms and handlebar moustache complementing his appearance. Sometimes he would be accompanied by a man on stilts, who, naturally, had to wait outside.

In the summer, the town's friendships were more evident. The French exchange students from Bayeux arrived in droves, easily recognisable in their long cotton scarves and drainpipe jeans. There was a neatness to their casualness, a nascent sophistication we couldn't hope to match. Even at fourteen, they all smoked Gauloises or Gitanes, with a coolness that suggested they had been smoking since birth. We sold these cigarettes too, but only to the handful of Francophile smokers, the aspiring Serge Gainsbourgs of the town.

My *correspondante* was Catherine Le Roy, an ideal match. Her parents ran a boulangerie and pâtisserie in Bayeux. We have stayed in touch over the years and visited her there, stopping off en route to family holidays in the South of France. Her shop was all glass and neatness, refined and minimalist compared to ours. It too was a sensory treat, with rows of glazed fruit tarts, and the aroma of fresh baguettes. Her father, Jean Pierre, baked through the night, emerging in the morning, his six o'clock shadow showing at 6am. Later she moved to Rouen, where she studied for *le Bac*. My sister and I attended her wedding, a convivial affair, where we were dubbed *les excentriques anglaises*, being the only guests wearing hats.

Working in the shop in the winter, when it was dark by four o'clock, was a totally different experience. Customers suddenly and mysteriously appeared out of the gloom. The first that you would know of their presence would be a gloved hand on the brass bar or a shadowy face at the door. Sometimes, the first sign you would have of their approach would be when the bell rang and the door opened to reveal them. Each customer arrived as if by surprise. Who would it be, a regular or a stranger?

Looking out into the darkness made you lose your bearings. You could be anywhere in the world. My mind played tricks on me. It felt easy to imagine our shop as a starship with space travellers stopping by for supplies before disappearing off at warp speed to some distant galaxy. People came in then melted away into the night. It made me apprehensive to go outside in case what I had imagined was real.

On rainy days, people dashed for cover, moaning about the weather, shaking sodden umbrellas outside and pulling wet hoods off their faces. The rain and darkness dampened moods.

Customers became impatient to get away as if being out in the weather was something unnatural. 'Once I'm home I'm not going out again, not in this weather!' they would say.

The transaction of buying and selling seemed more complex. People wearing woollen mittens fumbled for coins. Women in clear plastic headscarves protecting their perms dripped raindrops onto their purses as they tipped their heads forward to search for change. Elderly gentlemen searched blindly inside buttoned coats for the wallet in their breast pocket. Sometimes there was even a mini-undressing and re-dressing, before they ventured out into the dark cold again.

When we had closed up shop and emerged onto the street, the remnants of the passers-by seemed to have added haste to their step. In the summer people would have been happy to stop and chat; in the winter, they hurried home, necks drawn down into their collars like turtles.

Pa and I set off for the short walk down to the car park. We might pass the fruit and veg sellers, the father and son, in a procession of two empty barrows making their heavy way down Durngate Street. They were on their way to the lockup for the night, ahead of an early start the next morning with replenished stock.

'Night, Barry. Night, Neville.'

'Night, Clive. Keep warm.'

'I'm glad we don't have to work outside,' I thought to myself as I got into the car and whacked the heater on high. 'Ma will be cooking up a roast. Can't wait.'

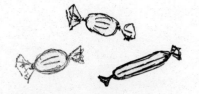

11

A Shop For All Occasions

VALENTINE'S DAY, EASTER, Mother's Day and Christmas were our busiest times. We needed to be ready with specialist cards and gifts and chocolates that people could buy as presents. Everything was hand-selected and ordered well in advance.

Although Valentine's cards were all different sizes, if you stood back from the display you would soon realise that most were bright red with a picture of hearts or kissing couples. It was always interesting to see which ones customers chose. They had the choice of the big padded box cards, 'To my darling fiancé', 'For my gorgeous husband', 'With love to my wife', or those with just the words 'Be mine!' on the front. I wondered whether the cards bought for 'my gorgeous husband' were reciprocated with the ones for 'my gorgeous wife', and how the requests to 'Be my Valentine' were received. And for the customers who bought more than one card, who was it they loved the most?

Working in the card shop at this time could be heartbreaking. A boy I had a crush on came in to buy a Valentine's card for his girlfriend. Sliding the card off the counter and placing it in a white paper bag, I avoided eye contact until the last minute.

Grazing his hand as I gave him his change was the extent of any intimacy with him that I would ever have.

After the big bright red hearts of Valentine's Day, Easter cards offered a more reflective selection. Images of skipping lambs and fluffy rabbits, waddling ducks and eggs in baskets, nestled amongst the poignant Bible verses. And just as the buying of a Christmas card doesn't imply the sender is religious, Easter cards were popular whatever the state of faith. The message then from the sender, not necessarily an acknowledgement of salvation, but that welcome spring had arrived.

For a man who enjoyed maths and puzzles, the Easter egg season was welcomed by Pa as a game. The challenge: to buy the correct number of Easter eggs so that when we closed the door after trading on the Saturday, there wouldn't be a single Easter egg left in the shop – or down in the cellar. The key was not to sell out too early or be left holding too many. It was a mathematical conundrum, Pa basing his estimate on a mixture of what we managed to sell last year, and what his gut told him about how many we would sell this year. There was no head office dictating numbers or targets, this challenge was entirely of his own making. The ordering, of course, took place months before Easter, the stock arriving en masse just after Christmas, like a bountiful production from a huge flock of chocolate laying hens.

As with every delivery, all the Easter eggs came in through the front door, the same door that the customers used right off the street. Deliveries would arrive on an unspecified day in January, when the first you would know about it would be when a lorry driver bearing an invoice announced, 'I've got five hundred Easter eggs for you in the van, where do you want them?'

If it was a Monday, Pa's day off, Ma would call him at home. 'The eggs have arrived, Clive, can you come in?' she would say down the phone, followed by an exasperated, 'Why do they always arrive when he's not here?' The delivery driver would be directed to pile them up in the narrow passageway beyond the till. Back and forth he would come, a constant stream of "Scuse me!' as he unloaded his van and weaved his way through the forward facing customers.

Pa would come in straight away and carry the boxes, four or five at a time, down to the cellar. It was a skilful balancing act negotiating the narrow wooden stairs while carrying a fragile tower of eggs. He couldn't see where he was going as the boxes exceeded the height of his head. Bending at his knees, keeping his back straight, allowing the heels of his polished tan leather shoes to lift off the floor, he would gently stand up, steadying the stack against his Roman nose. He would repeat the procedure tens of times until all the eggs were placed in the larder-like coolness of the cellar below.

The Easter eggs, hollow eggs with a few chocolates inside, were relatively light. But the heaviest were the boxes of mini eggs that we sold by the quarter pound. One day in January when Pa wasn't around, seventy boxes of Suchard mini praline eggs were delivered. Ma took on the challenge, carrying them down to the cellar, each box weighing close to six and a half pounds. She went home half dead.

We stored the eggs in the part of the cellar that had been the old kitchen when the shop had been a tea room. Here they would have baked a constant stream of scones and teacakes, sponge cakes and fondant fancies. Under our care it became a room full of chocolate eggs, a sprawling stack, which, once the run-up to Easter started, got smaller and smaller until the boxes became isolated and just a few remained. It seemed a fitting legacy, to continue the tradition of sweet treats, not dietary staples but tantalising mouthfuls that teased and delighted.

As Easter approached we unpacked the boxes and displayed their contents in the shop. The heavy sweet jars were taken off the shelves and reduced by half to make room to allow us to be over-run with Easter eggs. This was a time when you bought your Easter eggs at a sweet shop. There was Woolworths just along the street and a small supermarket further down the road, but the selection there was limited, so our shop became a Mecca for Easter egg hunters. The entire shop was taken over by them, as if all the hens had gone demented and switched to laying chocolate eggs. We had such a wonderful choice. If you didn't have someone to buy an egg for, you might just be tempted to buy one anyway.

Each year Pa would buy a spectacular centrepiece for our Easter themed shop window. It was usually the size of an ostrich egg, filled with tiny eggs, laid in a wicker basket, swathed in satin ribbons and bows and wrapped in cellophane. It was always a feather in the cap for the person who sold that one, which was mostly Mrs Eyres if I remember right.

Customers would gather up their choice of eggs from around the shop, presenting them to us at the till, arms laden. 'I'll have these, Clive, and have you got any more of those chocolate nests of mini eggs with the little yellow fury chick sat on top? The children so loved those last year.'

'I'll have a look,' he would say, disappearing off down into the cellar and returning either with the confectionery in his hand or an apologetic expression on his face.

Once the large eggs had gone, the race was on to sell the rest. Ideally we wanted to keep a range of prices to suit everyone's needs. Some years we would be left with just the small Cadbury's chocolate buttons or Smartie eggs, which weren't what the late-buying husbands or boyfriends were after.

Sometimes we would sell out so quickly that I would forget that I needed to buy my own; milk chocolate for Caroline, Suchard pralines for Pa and something completely different for Ma, usually scented toiletries.

In the years that we would sell out of eggs too early, Pa would offer customers one of our large boxes of chocolates instead, with the promise that, 'Lucinda will gift wrap it for you.' So I would set to work with the huge paper roll and industrial-sized Sellotape dispenser. The candy pink and white paper with *Osmond's Tobacconist & Confectioner* written in swirly ribbon-like calligraphy made a whipping sound as sheets got torn off. It was very much a while-you-wait service, and sometimes I would have a backlog of half a dozen boxes of chocolates to wrap, hurrying to do a neat job while not keeping the customers waiting too long.

'Here's another one for you, Lucinda. You're doing a grand job there!' Pa would say, as he piled up another box. Customers continued to shuffle in and out, the chirpy bell above the door ringing in time to their comings and goings.

Adjacent to the till and scales was a small shelf that at Easter was laden with boxes of loose little chocolate eggs, which we would weigh out and sell by the quarter or half pound in a white paper bag. They were more expensive than most of the sweets in jars, because they were special and seasonal. We sold Cadbury's mini eggs, pastel and speckled with a hard candy shell, but my favourites were the Lindt eggs, smooth melting chocolates in their regal foil jackets of vibrant purples, pinks and golds. Caroline loved the Suchard pralines, a bigger, nuttier mouthful in their patterned metallic wrappers. We were suckers for them all. Having them positioned by the till was just too tempting and easy to pick one as you went upstairs for your break, or as you squeezed past to look for stock in the cellar.

'Oy! That's our profit you're eating there!' Pa would say with a smile, as he took one for himself. Sometimes when the shop was quiet he would lob one at me with a 'Here, catch!' and I would hurriedly unwrap it and try to eat it before the next customer came in.

Some years Pa got his calculations right, some years he didn't. More often than not we sold out completely, save perhaps for a few of the smaller eggs. He needed to be accurate as eggs couldn't be returned to the supplier or kept for next year. No one wants to buy an Easter egg after Easter. The wrapping is such a large part of the cost of the egg, it's not cost efficient to break up the leftover eggs and sell them by the quarter pound. It was a bit like the card game Gin Rummy – any cards that you are left holding at the end of the game count against you. And so it was with Easter eggs.

At the end of trade on the final Saturday before Easter Sunday, Pa and I would close up and go along to the bar at the Antelope Hotel. Over a pint of Huntsman for him, and a half of lager and lime for me, we would share a packet of salt and vinegar crisps as we chatted about the customers and the fun of it all. If we had sold all the eggs, or been left with just a few, it felt like we had played the tables and beaten the casino again. One time he surprised me by speaking more seriously. 'Ma and I have been talking,' he said. 'When you are older, we could give the shops to you and Caroline. Perhaps you would like to have the sweet shop, and Caroline the cards?' I knew in an instant that it was not what I wanted, and I think that he did too. I had my heart set on nursing and Caroline, though still undecided, yearned to travel. We loved working in the shop, but knew it would not be like this forever. Our life plans involved leaving Dorchester, finding out about what the world had to offer. But although I did not want it, it was a privilege to have it offered. It was not my long-term dream, but I was reminded that while it lasted, this was our family business, created, worked and enjoyed by us. And that felt special indeed.

As Christmas approached, it wasn't just us, the whole street became festive. Christmas trees went up outside every shop, decorated with coloured lights. The barrows, decked with clumps of holly and mistletoe, sold seasonal dates and satsumas, large string bags of walnuts, and mounds of Brussels sprouts. The Town Crier in full regalia stood next to carol singers in full song.

In the sweet shop we stocked some lines that we only carried at Christmas, like Lindt Mountain Rose or large tins of Quality Street, hexagonal boxes of Turkish Delight and chocolate brazil nuts, in milk or plain. We also stocked Terry's Chocolate Orange, which some people bought to put in the foot of the Christmas stocking. It was a treat for us because we never saw these at any other time of the year.

There was a fighting spirit, a sense of shoppers on a mission sharing knowledge and words of advice. 'Don't bother going down the Post Office, they're queuing out the door,' someone would holler into the full shop.

And they queued with us too. There was an ebb and flow, the shop filling up to capacity and then briefly emptying again, while we did what we could in the moments of calm. Dashing down to the cellar for more stock, keeping the windows refreshed, or cleaning the trail of rainy footprints off the red marbled lino floor.

People staggered in, laden with bags, in hats and gloves, hampered by their heavy coats. They paid in cash or handwritten cheque, a credit card a rarity. But often in big notes, a fifty or a twenty, freshly pressed, from the monthly pay packet. Dashing out to the bank or down to Stuart Turner's for change, the pace of the day sped up. There was no time to stop to chat.

We were at full stretch, not only working flat out, but also at the bank. We had bought and paid for the goods in advance and now we had to sell them. As with the other seasonal stock, it has a limited window of desirability. We hoped we had what people wanted. Working with Ma and Pa was not stressful. I have known bosses who get anxious and take out their stress on their staff, but this wasn't the case with them. They treated it as a challenge, a game in which we all had our part to play.

We worked in tag teams serving customers or stocking up, getting as prepared as we could for the rush. In the card shop, our counter was set up by the door with one till, but at Christmas and at other busy times an extra till was set up to get paying customers out through the door as quickly as possible. The busiest times were in people's lunch breaks, when they rushed in to buy Christmas cards and catch up on their shopping. At these times the shop was full. We always said it was nice to be busy, but we appreciated the lull and space to breathe again.

Sometimes I would pop over and help out Julie or Ma, standing at the till while they went to restock the cards after the swarm. Some had missing envelopes, others were scattered where they shouldn't be. Most cards weren't cellophane wrapped, and each card had to be individually marked by hand. It was quite an art, fanning them out so that just the corners showed, and writing the price in pencil on the back. The cards in cellophane would be marked with a sticker from the kerplunker, our name for the clunky handheld pricing machine.

People readied themselves for the big day. The elderly women in their fresh purple perms, coiffed ready for Christmas, the younger women hot from the hairdressers, some with curlers still left in. There was a sense of a countdown, the women bearing the burden, under pressure to get everything done by Christmas Eve. Nowhere would be open until the day after Boxing Day, so there was no chance to buy anything forgotten.

'Are you ready for Christmas?' customers would ask each other.

And the replies they gave were always the same.

'Haven't bought a thing. I do my shopping on Christmas Eve,' from the men, and from the women, 'All this fuss for just one day!'

But it wasn't just another day. Tied in with the celebration of Christmas was an acknowledgement that the year was coming to an end. The New Year started over the page, and there was hope and longing for what it would bring. But amongst the joy was the counterpoint of sadness. The elderly seem to become more frail as the pages on the calendar run out, and their demise more likely. It is almost as if in December they take stock as to whether they have the energy in them for another year. Amongst the cards we sold, wishing merriness and joy, were also those offering messages of sympathy. While some people were celebrating, others were grieving. And not just those who grieved the newly departed, but those who relived their grief as the anniversary of departure came round again.

Running the shop gave us an intimacy with our customers' lives. More accessible than a priest, we witnessed their joys and challenges, their times of celebration. We knew their births, deaths, marriages, their anniversaries and confirmations. We knew when they were moving house, learning to drive or getting engaged. We knew their secrets too, their clandestine Valentines, or gifts of chocolates to make up after a row. All in all it was a unique insight into the everyday comings and goings of the people of Dorchester. Through the seasons we watched them meet their milestones; grow up, grow old and depart this life.

12

Customers & Characters

SOMEONE ONCE DESCRIBED Dorchester as a town with the countryside 'just over the rise'. And that's what it is. You are never far from countryside you can escape to, from rivers and streams you can walk by. At the entrance to the town from the east, the River Frome is crossed by Grey's Bridge. Locals used to say, 'He's never been further than Grey's Bridge,' which meant that someone who had been born and raised in the town had never been anywhere else. There were still some of the older people that you could say that about when we were living there. Some people you felt had not travelled very far at all.

If we had been a hairdressers, customers would have come in with overgrown locks in need of a cut. If we had been a launderette, people would have brought in piles of dirty washing. If we had been a chemist, customers would have come in, hacking and coughing, in search of a remedy. Each shop has its own culture of characters, and we, like them, had our own. We weren't like the hairdressers who only saw their customers every six to eight weeks. Some of our regulars came in every day, especially for cigarettes; chain-smokers cupping their hand around their lit stub to avoid making a hole in our lino. If the ash got too long they would dash to the door and tap it out into the street, to save burning their hands. People shopping with a fag in their mouths, lips stretched and head tipped back to help keep it in place, a lop-sided tension across their face, like a palsy. All chain-smoking, like the Olympic torch that never goes out, the last one lighting the next – the perpetual flame. Why such a habit? Bringing the first two fingers, closed together, to the pursed lips to draw on a cigarette is the same motion you would use to blow a kiss. With the cigarette, you pause to inhale, then blow the smoke away. With a kiss, you touch the fingertips to the lips, then blow the kiss away. No wonder smoking is so hard to quit, it can feel like you're in love.

But our regulars weren't just smokers, they also loved our sweets. People got into a rhythm to stop by; a pensioner with hair as white as the Mint Imperials she asked for, a half pound every week, came in without fail, whatever the weather, always unaccompanied. Did she live alone or just have a husband who didn't like to shop?

Wednesdays and Saturdays were the busiest days of the week for us, and for the town generally. Wednesday was market day and everyone came in to catch up with people they hadn't seen all week. You would see huddles of people in the street chatting and exchanging gossip and news. It was a ritual. The farmers arrived in green wellies and worn old corduroys puffed up at the knees where they had been sitting down, looking like they had just driven their tractor into town. Taking their time to buy their tinned tobacco, fumbling for coins in their numerous Barbour pockets. And the farmers' wives with baskets, always in a hurry, hand-knitted socks showing above their boots, ruddied complexions and hard worn hands, with a look on their faces that said, 'I've been up since dawn.' Women with pushchairs piled high with shopping, trying to stop their children from touching everything. And men who would ask for twenty

Bensons and give you a fistful of change, which you didn't need to count. Hands picking out pennies one at a time in kid gloves or bare workers' hands, muddied or oiled, some badly bitten to the quick; stubby chubby fingers more at home on the farm or long polished talons not used to physical work. Handfuls of change, ready counted and sorted, hot sweaty coins closely guarded, torn notes in need of first aid. And some hands that opened up and let you take what you needed, 'Go on, love, I've not got my glasses today.'

Children came in holding a shiny penny in their hand. Holding it up to my face, they would ask, 'Can I get anything for this?' as they looked longingly at the wall of weigh-out sweets. 'Well, not really. The smallest amount we sell at a time is two ounces, and that's about 7p. Have a look down there,' I would say, as I pointed to the shelf of penny chews. Then they would crouch, all knees and scruffy shoes, to spend every last ha'penny of their pocket money.

I always had an awareness of who else was in the shop, who was being served and who was to be next. Those being served would have their purses or wallets open, cash ready in their hand, looking attentive as if waiting to catch a barman's eye. 'I'll have a quarter of wine gums, please. Not too many green ones if you don't mind.'

The lads from Curry's across the road used to come in every day. Whenever there was a big televised sporting event on they would invite Pa over to enjoy the game in return for him bringing packets of peanuts and crisps. They got called 'The Likely Lads' because of their teasing quips.

'Half a pound of jelly babies, and make sure they're all boys because you get more jelly,' one of them would say.

'Well, that depends,' I would utter under my breath, wishing I had the nerve to be more bold.

At the entrance to the shop was a deadly two inch step that was to surprise our less frequent visitors. It was too small to be noticeable and so unless they knew it was there, they could catch their foot on it as they entered the threshold, causing them to be propelled forward into the shop at a sudden jolt, like a paper aeroplane. All we could do was stand powerless as the customer arrived at a higher velocity than intended, arms immovable at their sides with their nose pointed skywards in an effort to direct their projection away from the beckoning ground. Regaining their composure, they would inevitably act as though such an entrance was exactly as planned, and make their buying choice once they had caught their breath. Fortunately, there were never any casualties or serious injuries, and over the years, although it was clearly no laughing matter, we could not help but see the funny side of such episodes. It was yet another example of how our customers kept us entertained.

Some customers we got to know pretty well, while others remained a mystery. One of our customers who liked to chat was Frank who worked in the dry cleaners and moonlighted at the chip shop. He was bald. Wanting to appear younger than his lack of hair made him look, he set about getting himself a wig. He travelled down to Southampton by train, to a wig shop recommended by a friend. He chose one and decided to wear it on the journey home. It wasn't until he got up from his seat on the train back to Dorchester that he caught his reflection in the window. To his horror, his entire head of hair was standing on end. The warm rush of air from the train's arrival had played havoc with the nylon fibres and created static of the most extreme kind.

'I thought people were looking at me a bit funny,' he told Ma.

'You've given up on it now then?' she asked, looking up at his bald head.

'Yeah, that was just a fancy. The wife will have to take me as I am.'

After a slight hesitation she asked, 'Are you any good with mice?'

'What, as a pet?'

'No!' she replied, and then more quietly, 'Getting rid of them.'

'You've got mice?' he asked.

'Yes. Clive found a handful of bars that had been nibbled at. He's laid a trap. Come down the cellar with me.'

'Oh Mrs O, now there's an offer!' and then after a pause he added, 'I don't really like mice.'

Ignoring his response, Ma took hold of his hand and led him down the wooden steps to the cellar below.

'Look down there under that stool, that's where we laid the trap,' she said. 'See if there's anything in it.'

Frank stooped to bend down, the bare cellar lightbulb reflecting in the back of his shiny head.

'Not sure I like live ones!' he said as he leapt up onto the stool.

'What are you doing up there?' Ma asked, looking up at him and then down at the ground. 'I think it's dead,' she said as she went in for closer inspection. Frank got down off the stool and gingerly picked up the sprung wooden trap with the decaying, crushed creature attached.

'I think you're right,' he said with arm outstretched and holding his breath. 'He's a goner.'

Fortunately for Frank, the mice were kept at bay and he never again got asked to retrieve a trap. His role as mouse-catcher was as short lived as his brief flirtation with his hairpiece.

One of our more enigmatic customers was a man who called himself Lord Bingham, supposed cousin of the disappeared Lord Lucan. He too was a mystery. He wore a black cape with red satin lining over a pinstripe suit, and carried a silver-tipped walking cane and top hat. His dark hair was slicked back with Brylcreem, and he held himself with ramrod erectness. The only things out of place were his misaligned front teeth.

He used to say he didn't drive, relying instead on his chauffeur-driven Rolls-Royce. We only ever saw him on Wednesdays, the day the market bus came into town.

'He's no more a Lord than I'm a Lady!' said one of our customers.

He used to come in just as we were closing, particularly around the time of Charles and Diana's wedding in 1981. He wanted a wedding gift proportionate to his social standing, something bespoke. Could we help? We put him in touch with one of our suppliers. We never saw the final gift or heard how it was received by the royal couple. I don't think we had a chance to ask. Like his errant relation, he then disappeared.

Another perplexing character was a man we met late one Saturday afternoon, when Pa and I were getting ready to close up. We noticed him hanging around outside, eyeing up the cigar window. He stood with his shoulders hunched, hands deep in the pockets of his grey gabardine mac, with a belt that was tied too tight. His greying hair was severely parted and lying flat on his head.

Pa went outside to ask him if he wanted anything as we were closing. The man followed Pa into the shop, his watery eyes seeming to lack focus. He said he wanted a lighter. Well, he was in the right place. We had every type of cigarette or pipe lighter you could possibly want. A chrome Ronson variety with a flick metal cover like in the James Bond films, disposable Bic lighters, or novelty lighters with what looked like feathers floating around in them. This last one is what had caught this customer's eye.

'That'll be 99p then, please, sir,' said Pa, as the man counted out the exact money and headed off into the darkness, down the street.

The following Saturday he appeared again, loitering outside at closing time.

'There's that man again, Pa, the one with the lighter,' I said.

'He's not here again, is he? You go out and see what he wants.'

Out I went only to be told that he wanted another lighter.

'It is refillable, you know, we sell the cans of lighter fuel. You don't need to buy a new lighter every time,' I explained. There came no reply, except a request for another lighter just like the one he had bought last week.

On the third week, he was there again.

'What is going on with that man?' I asked Pa. 'What is he doing with his lighters?'

'Perhaps he's collecting them, or losing them. Didn't you tell him they're refillable?'

Pa invited the man in only to repeat the same transaction again.

On the fourth week, lighter man appeared once more, only this time he was accompanied, by a male nurse from the local psychiatric hospital.

'Mr Osmond, please don't sell this man any more lighters. We've had to confiscate them. He's been lighting his cigarettes under the bed clothes. This last time he set his bed on fire – he's lucky to be here now. As am I.'

Pa and I both stood staring at the diminutive figure in front of us, the realisation dawning that we really knew very little about the secret lives of our customers.

We were aware of our neighbours in the town; the father and son working the barrows just up the street outside Boots, selling their fruit and vegetables in all weathers; the quietly spoken owner of Templeman's, the leather goods shop where our school satchels came from and, later, a pair of red calf-leather driving gloves we bought Pa as a Christmas present. And the magician and his assistant, and most probably a company of disappearing rabbits, who lived above Frisby's shoe shop.

Someone else we got to know well was Stuart Turner, the tobacconist and confectioner in Tudor Arcade, just across the road. I suppose you could say that he and Pa shouldn't have been friends – they were rivals, but their easy-going personalities and common interests got in the way of that. In fact, they helped each other out hugely. If we ran out of a brand of tobacco or needed change, one of us would pop down to Stuart's to get some while Pa kept the customer talking. Likewise, Stuart knew he could come to us if he was in need.

Stuart was warm and well spoken, with a smile and relaxed manner that reflect a man who has his priorities right. He knew how to put people at ease, which is probably why he was a welcome presence in the town for so many years. By the time we arrived in Dorchester, Stuart had been trading as a confectioner and tobacconist for thirteen years, after his father set him up in business. Within a few months of our arrival, Stuart had grown a beard and started wearing a Guernsey sweater, just like Pa.

Many an evening after closing we would walk down the arcade past Stuart's shop to see him still there, leaning against the counter, talking to a customer. We would catch his eye and he would acknowledge us with a wave and a wink. It was a fitting end to the day, shutting up shop and saying goodnight to the best friend in town.

Pa and Stuart were both in the Lions, like many of the business people in Dorchester. It was an organisation whose principal aim was raising money for local causes and charities, but they also managed to have incredible fun. One summer they put on a sponsored raft race, not down the river as you might expect, but down South Walks. Teams built wooden rafts on castors that they then punted down the path with broom handles. It was a hilarious sight, not least because they all came dressed as pirates, a ramshackle bunch in frayed trousers and eye patches, laughing so much they hardly had the strength to push.

Judging by the stack of black and white photos, Pa used to love fancy dress. One of my favourites is of him dressed as a chimney sweep, a young man, beardless, with rakish grin, a tied handkerchief at his neck and gaiters bound with string over his hobnail boots. How odd it is to see photos of your parents when they are young, of an age you never witnessed. It is wonderful to see them enjoying themselves, having fun with their friends.

Stuart had a boat, and he used to invite Pa and some of the other Lions friends out for sailing trips from Poole Harbour. Pa enjoyed the sociability of it, although he didn't have the sea legs to be a good sailor. The mistake was usually starting the beery picnic too early. By the time they got out of the calm of the harbour and into the open sea, the choppy waters started to have an effect and Pa would be found chucking up over the back of the boat.

'I'll turn back if you give me your business, Clive.'

'Never! Keep going,' Pa said between retches, 'it'll take more than this!'

Stuart and Pa were to come across each other on a less sociable occasion. For the most part, customers paid for their goods promptly. We had regulars who would come in while you were serving someone else who would leave the exact money on the side of the till. They would help themselves to the packs of cigarettes they were after, catch your eye, and intimate with a nod that, 'The money's on the side.'

There were a few other customers who would ask to buy things on tick. It was a practice we inherited from the previous owners. Some customers expected it, so to begin with, we went along with it. After a while, though, we realised that allowing the practice was the quickest way to lose customers. Wising up, Pa explained to me one day, 'Never let anyone have anything on tick. They'll get behind with their bills, and won't be able to pay. Then they will be too embarrassed to come in, and you'll never see them again.'

But there were some who seemed reluctant to play by the rules. One of these was a woman who used to help herself to packs of cigarettes.

'Put it on the slate,' she would call as she hurried for the door. 'I'll settle up at the end of the month.'

'Wait a minute!' Pa would call, but she would be gone.

The next time she came in, Pa might just have a chance to ask, 'You haven't forgotten your bill, have you?'

'No, of course, I won't let you down. I'll pay you next week,' she would say.

Next week came, and she never paid. Then she stopped coming into the shop altogether. A few weeks later, Pa saw her coming out of Stuart Turner's. Pa decided enough was enough.

Fortunately, Pa knew where she lived. She had given her address when she had initially started getting things on tick. One night after closing up, he drove round to her flat. He parked up outside with the lights off and waited for her to come home from work. While there, he noticed another car with the driver sitting inside, also with its lights off. After a while the woman arrived home and went into her flat. As Pa got out of his car he noticed the other driver do the same. It was Stuart.

'You're not here as well, are you?' Pa asked.

'I certainly am. She's not getting any more out of me.'

The traders you came across at the market were different from the shopkeepers in the town. Men and women on a perpetual tour of pitches and plots, trading stock, bartering and bantering; men in heavy sheepskin coats selling rugs out of a converted ice cream van; a solitary woman standing silently behind a picnic table of car accessories or jewellery pots; and young lads with cheeky smiles selling saucy underwear. And then there were the showmen, the artful traders that could sell anyone anything.

One day Caroline and I saw a transit van with its doors wide open spilling its contents onto the ground; electrical goods that had fallen off the back of a lorry, we presumed. Two traders dressed in Levi's and scruffy T-shirts eyed the punters as they passed. The men piled up desirable items around the open door of the van, and a crowd began to gather, eager for a bargain. To one side was a pile of boxes, sealed and unlabelled. At the other side, a handful of televisions, transistor radios, cassette players. As the audience grew, the show began.

'Who's up for a gamble? Who's up for a bit of fun?' the market trader asked.

'I've got all these boxes but I don't know what's in them. Who'll give me a pound for a punt?'

Then someone stepped forward, breaking the silence. 'I will,' he said, proffering his pound coin, his facial features bearing a striking resemblance to the showman. But the attentive crowd seemed not to notice, distracted by the things on show.

'Good on you, sir. Here's yours.'

Then encouraged, other people standing round stepped forward.

'I'll take one.'

'And me.'

'Go on then,' says another, as each in turn gave up their money in exchange for a secret box.

There we were, caught in the crowd, drawn by the patter, strangely alluring. Caroline had a pound burning a hole in her pocket.

'Shall I buy one?'

'Well, you don't know what's inside.'

'It might be good.'

'Could be.'

She stepped forward with her money and took the box. Walking away she opened it: a glass fish ornament with protuberant lips, flecked with daubs of spattered paint.

'Oh,' she said. 'What am I going to do with this?'

'Give it to Ma as a present.'

And she did. It lived in Ma's bathroom until we moved house. An elegant room with avocado corner bath, plush pile carpet, the height of contemporary style and design. And on the shelf, a painted glass fish that Ma couldn't bear to bin.

13

Ma & Grandma

How do you describe your mother? Someone you know so well, yet are so used to their wants and their ways that they are no longer remarkable. It is a bit like shopping for trinkets on holiday: once you have seen them a hundred times you stop finding them of interest. It is only when you get back home from your trip that you realise they were rather special, and wished you had some to keep.

Despite the childhood photographs of her in a bathing suit on the beach, with puppy fat and tussled hair, it is still hard for me to imagine her as young. Yet the wilful twinkle in her dark eyes connects like a thread through all the images of her I have ever seen.

And wilful she was. 'If you told me not to do something, I'd have to do it,' she says.

'Don't touch that, Judith!' my grandmother Marjorie would say. 'I'll get the stick down.' Then locking looks with her, Ma's large brown eyes holding her gaze, like two birds of prey after the same meal, Ma would reach out slowly and lightly touch the forbidden thing, deluded in her belief that the glacial speed of her movement would somehow camouflage her action.

Punishment followed swiftly; a stinging whip to her calves

from the cane kept behind the picture of the Highland Glen in the front room. Sometimes, for penance, she would be locked in the under-stairs cupboard. She would sit in the dark, eyes and ears alert for movement, listening out for footsteps on the string of flagstones in the hall, waiting for a change in the beat of her mother's step. Would this be the time she stops and opens the door, letting in a shaft of angular light from the day outside?

And sometimes it was.

'Are you sorry yet?' Grandma would ask of the darkness.

And though Ma so desperately wanted to say, 'Yes,' and to be cuddled and forgiven, the word changed shape in her mouth and she heard herself spit, 'No!'

'Well, you're staying in there then!'

The door would close on her once more and she would sit alone again, settling herself back onto the ragbag of sackcloth full of worn-out clothes such as her father's old plus fours. Sometimes she would sing, a further act of defiance. One time she fell asleep, and gave Grandma the fright of her life. She thought that she had been suffocated. Sometimes I would be sent on an errand at my grandma's house to the cupboard under the stairs and I would try to imagine as I clicked open the triangular wooden door, bending down into the sloping space, what it would be like spending time in there alone in the dark. I didn't hesitate long, getting in and out quickly, the space smelling of shoe polish and oily dusters, a place meant only for storage of the vacuum cleaner and old rags.

When Ma was slightly older, aged about seven, she packed her little case with a change of clothes and her favourite toy.

'I'm leaving home,' she declared to my grandmother, turning her back and walking towards the porch. 'Off you go then,' Marjorie replied.

Out the door she went, checking behind her after every few steps. Getting halfway down the road, she stopped to pause behind a lamp post, expecting Grandma to come running towards her, pleading with her to come back. She never did, no one did. After waiting a while longer she returned home, unpacked her little suitcase and decided that today was not the best day to leave home after all.

Ma was the same age as Pa, being just two years old at the outbreak of war. Whereas Pa was evacuated to safety like so many thousands of children, Ma, who lived in Exeter at the time, stayed put with the family. Unlike London, Exeter had been considered an unlikely bombing target. Yet bombing raids became a frequent occurrence in the city, including the Baedeker raid on 4 May 1942, so called after the travel guide of the same name, when the centre of Exeter was obliterated. Forty bombers flattened the centre, leaving 161 people dead and 476 injured. Ma remembers hearing the news that thirty people alone were killed in the Royal Mail sorting office that night.

Early in the war when the sirens sounded, Grandpa Wilson would hurry Ma and her older sister and his wife Marjorie into the Austin 7 and drive into the country lanes outside Exeter. They would park under cover of trees and sit and wait in silence with the car lights turned off, the children dressed in siren suits, little zip-up hooded pyjamas worn with boots to keep their feet warm. They sat as a family in the darkness watching the sky light up, keeping silent, keeping still, much like the Von Trapp family trying not to be noticed by the Nazis. They were lucky they had a car and that Wilson was around to drive them as Marjorie didn't drive. Wilson was in his early thirties at the start of the war and received his call-up papers but, as a butcher, was made exempt from active duty by the Ministry of Food.

Later in the war when they heard the sirens, they headed off to the Anderson shelter at the bottom of the garden that my grandfather and a friend had built one Sunday afternoon. They had dug a great hole and inserted upright wooden posts to support a piece of domed corrugated metal; an incongruous igloo-shaped hut amidst the vegetable plot. It had wooden steps leading down to it. From there you could watch the bombs dropping and the sky light up. Some of Ma's friends without gardens had a Morrison shelter, an iron table that stayed in the house that people crouched under.

One day when the siren had sounded and they had all got to safety inside the shelter, my grandmother got up announcing, 'I have to go back in the house, I've got a cake in the oven.' Despite rationing, she had managed to get hold of two fresh eggs to make a Victoria sponge for Ma's birthday and she wasn't about to let it spoil. She climbed out and ran back into the house, sirens blaring, all eyes from the shelter fixed on her. She had risked her life for a cake, but both survived safe and sound.

Their home was never hit by bombs but Ma remembers other houses nearby being destroyed. Bodies were laid out in the street in rows, covered with a coat or blanket with just their feet showing.

Grandma Marjorie was in service from the age of fourteen, working at a big house across Bodmin Moor. She started out as a maid, later becoming a cook, walking five miles across the fields to get to work. She had just a half day off a week, but even then she had to get all her jobs done before she could leave, blacking the grates and relaying the coal fires.

I used to watch her clean and set the coal fire in her home, holding up a wide sheet of newspaper over the gap in the hearth to let the fire draw, like bringing a huge monster to life. I am sure that if I had done it I would have set fire to the paper, but she did it so skilfully, almost without conscious thought, a skill practised over many years.

And when I set a fire now, as I bend down onto my knees I never fail to think of her as a young unmarried woman, setting her fire with skill in haste to finish her chores before leaving the great house, to stride across the moors to start her half day off.

Coming into the stone cottage, up the worn polished steps, taking off her muddy boots and kissing her mother, my great-grandmother Lizzie, on her cheek, who would smell of home cooking and soap just like Grandma did.

Marjorie's main role in life, that I could see, was feeding the family and she was very good at it. Knowing the importance she placed on food made me value it more. Not only the appreciation of her efforts at her well-practised repertoire of recipes, all prepared without a single cookery book, but that food is precious and not to be wasted. It was a hangback to her growing up on a farm where food was strongly linked to survival. She enjoyed food, but she knew that sometimes it was hard to come by.

Marjorie used to help feed the animals on her mother's farm, and one of them, a duck named Billy, used to follow her around wherever she went. It was like having a pet, she used to say, he followed her everywhere.

'What happened to him, Grandma?' we asked her one day.

'We ate him I expect, at Christmas.'

It was a response my sister and I could never understand. The very thought of eating Starsky and Hutch, Caroline's guinea pigs, or Snoopy, our cat, was beyond comprehension.

'How could you do that?' we asked.

'Things were different then,' she said, 'everything had to earn its keep.'

She was a wonderful cook. If she had been baking she would have a light powdering of flour on her cheeks. When you went to kiss her you would pick up the fragrance of lily of the valley soap, which in the summer months got mingled with the scent of sweet peas from her garden. Cornish pasties and buns were her speciality, she must have made those every week. Whenever I was coming over to see her, she would make me junket, ''specially', served in a small cut glass bowl with cream that she had whisked by hand. Both were covered with little circles of net bordered by a ring of dangling buttons that she had sewn herself, to keep off the flies. It tasted delicious, like nothing else I had ever had.

She had a budgerigar called Peter, and would open up his cage and let him enjoy a good swoop about the room, before inviting him back to his newly cleaned quarters with a fresh supply of seed and cuttlefish. She was quite like a bird herself, petite and alert, moving purposefully without expending excessive movement.

There were signs of girlishness in her dress. She loved hats, and never went out without one or, on warmer days, a silk headscarf square. She would wear plain felt hats or slightly furry ones that perhaps had some mohair in them. Then she would embellish them with a fold of grosgrain or satin ribbon kept in place by a decorative silver button picked from the button tin, which I think once upon a time may have been a tea caddy.

This was the generation of adult women who never wore trousers, wore stockings never tights, and having grown up without central heating were masters at using layers to keep warm. Fine-knit woolly vests, worn even in July and August, and full length slips and cardigans were the mainstays of their wardrobes. The generation whose home-life uniform were not onesies or tracksuit pants but a Bri-Nylon knee-length button-front overall. Her's was in lemon.

Watching television programmes with Grandma was accompanied by her running commentary on the current life status of the actors. Pointing at the screen she would say, 'What are you watching this for? He's dead, she's dead, all dead and gone.' Then she would get up from her chair, rubbing her arthritic knee and go out to the kitchen to find something useful to do.

What I saw as funny, her odd, old ways, were part of her acute awareness of her age and the value of life. As I laughed and thought, 'Oh Grandma,' I had forgotten that she had lost her father, her mother and her brother. In that nuclear family she was the only one left. Her outbursts as she watched images of spent lives came from the belief that it doesn't serve to dwell on the past. The present is all we have.

Walking back to her house with Caroline one day, enjoying the sense of family, I remember saying, 'I hope you live to be a hundred, Grandma.'

'Oh I don't,' she replied quickly, as if she had made up her mind about that some time ago. 'I don't want to get old. I don't want to be doddery and dribbling. I hope I pass away in my sleep.'

Her response shocked me and my sister. How could anyone not want to live as long as they possibly could? But when the time came, she got her wish.

One day when she was in her late sixties she disappeared. I remember the rumpus she caused, the concern and confusion. She couldn't drive, she never went anywhere far without Grandpa. I remember the pow-wow of perplexed looks, the grave concern as he, my mother and aunt asked the same question, 'Where could she have gone?'

And then, she just came home, walking in through the front door and hanging up her hat as if she had just popped out to the postbox. It turned out that she had taken the bus to Weston-super-Mare, about an hour and a half away, to sit on the beach, giving herself a day off from baking and cooking, cleaning and sewing.

'Good for you, Grandma,' I thought as I looked on admiringly, the gumption, the guts, the suntanned face. She had made her point.

At the age of seventy-two Grandma became a poet. After spending three days recovering in hospital from treatment for trigeminal neuralgia (a condition that causes excruciating facial nerve pain), when she didn't know who or where she was or recognise any of her family, she made a complete recovery and took to writing poetry. One of her favourite poems was published in a magazine (I've included it at the end of this book). Up until then I had never known her write a line, except of course for her letter writing. She was a loyal correspondent, writing regularly to friends and family, and to me when I left home, on Basildon Bond in duck egg blue. Where her passion for poetry came from I have no idea. Perhaps, like her trip to Weston and her desire for adventure, it was something that could only be repressed for so long. Why not start at seventy-two? As long as you have breath, it is never too late.

She used to speak very little about herself, but if she could be persuaded she would always start off in the same way. 'I'm Marjorie, just Marjorie. They didn't think to give me a middle name.'

Marjorie Bunt, Grandma, picking sweet peas
in her garden at 59 Prince of Wales Road, Dorchester.

14

Friendships & Fun

WITHOUT REALLY NOTICING, our bikes had to go when we moved to live above the shop because we had nowhere to store them. We had no garage or garden shed. We had no garden. In Weymouth we used to ride our bikes along the prom, where I had learned to cycle. Pa, the eternal engineer, had of course devised the perfect learning aid, an adaptation to my two-wheeler of a soldered stub of metal fixed to the base of my saddle onto which he slotted a length of hollow pipe about two feet long. He used to run behind me, holding onto the metal rod as I pedalled, and then as I became more confident and with gathering speed, he pulled off the snugly fitting pipe and let me ride away from him on two wheels. I knew when he was running behind me, I could hear the chafe of his jacket and jangle of coins in his pocket. As I became more proficient, cycling along trying to keep the handlebars straight, I realised through the veil of my concentration that Pa was no longer behind me. All I could hear was the turn of the pedals and the repetitive spin of my tyres. 'Keep going, Lucinda, you've got it!' he yelled from afar. When I finally lost my nerve and reached for the brakes, I turned to look behind. There, running towards me, rod in hand, beaming at my success, was Pa.

I only realise now the pain and guilt my parents felt, particularly my mother, during the years we lived above the shop. She hated the fact that we had no garden to play in. To be honest, I don't remember it bothering my sister and me at all. We spent most of our free time playing in the garden of our friends' house, who lived in Trinity Street, the road that ran parallel behind our shop. There were four of them, Kate, Sarah, Vicky and Nicko Seaton, the two eldest nearest in age to Caroline and me. Even when we turned up unannounced, we would find ourselves with enthusiastic playmates, eager to share their games and latest discoveries. Theirs was a homely Georgian house that you entered right off the street. Pushing open the heavy gloss door, which never seemed to be locked, was a magical experience. High airy ceilings, large rooms and what felt like a secret garden. Stepping onto the huge lawn we would play tag, or with two of us holding a length of rope, we would challenge each other to see who could jump the highest. Barefoot, lithe limbs, skirts tucked up into our knickers, we would push ourselves to the limit. Stepping back into the flowerbeds to take a long run up, hurling ourselves over the rope. We would fall on the grass, fearless of injury, egging each other on to jump higher and higher.

One of the more exuberant games was to jump down the stairs from the top landing. The idea was to take a running jump and leap from the corridor, over the stairs below and land on the narrow half landing missing the stairs and without flattening yourself on the wall. I don't know how we managed it. If we had landed on the stairs, it would have been a very unforgiving fall.

We would alternate with less energetic activities, going upstairs to their play room, riding their full-sized rocking horse, or attempting to play 'Chopsticks' on their grand piano.

Sometimes we would just sit and play a board game. In the summer holidays when we had exhausted all that Dorchester had to offer, their mum would pile us into the back of their Peugeot estate and take us off to the bigger towns of Poole or Bournemouth to the swimming baths or ice rink. Caroline and I spent hours with them, soaking up the entertainment, stopping only for quenching drinks or gobbled lunch of creamy chicken and rice. It was our kids' camp, adventure playground, our sports day, all rolled into one.

When friends weren't around we made our own fun. On the outside wall of our shop, our local cinema, the Plaza, advertised its latest films. In return, we got complimentary cinema tickets. This was brilliant for Caroline and me. We didn't have to show a pass, we had no card, just saying, 'We get free tickets, we're from Osmond's,' was enough to see us ushered in without paying. On rainy days or when we were at a loose end, we could just pop up to the cinema on Trinity Street and watch a film for free. Our favourite was *The Sound of Music*. We must have seen that a dozen times. Quite often we would have the place to ourselves, soaking up the faded grandeur of the Art Deco building. We would sit up in the gods, with only them for company, enjoying the Salzburg countryside and Maria's inner wrangling of love over duty. Our favourite bit was when we could sing along to Mother Abbess singing 'Climb Ev'ry Mountain' to Maria.

There was no Dolby sound and the seats were covered in a faded velvet that was so old it had become prickly to sit on in anything other than full length trousers. But it was like having our own private screening, perfect for when we just wanted to get away from people and enjoy some escapism for a while. However, with time, there was a downside to getting free tickets – what to tell boyfriends who, as was customary for the first date, suggested a trip to the cinema. I'm guessing that most conversations between mothers and daughters back then on the subject of boys and first dates to the cinema would be about what to do if he suggested sitting in the back row. For us, we discussed at length whether to come clean about the free tickets. Ma, still having some vague medieval notion that the age of chivalry was still thriving in Britain, was convinced that any such confession would cause the unsuspecting boy despair, and erosion of his manhood.

'You can't tell him,' she pleaded. 'He will lose face and be embarrassed. All boys expect to pay on the first date.'

My sister and I would share a glance, trying to visualise this chivalrous world to which Ma referred. Chivalry in Dorchester in 1979? Doors being held open for us? Capes laid across puddles? Personalised poetry sent by special messenger? No. We didn't know any boys who behaved like that.

But, perhaps she knew better than us. Invariably, we gave in, agreeing with her strategy and joining in with this imagined fantasy land. We would collude to keep quiet and let the boy maintain his dignity and pay for the tickets, even though we could get in for free.

However, we hadn't counted on Shirley in the cinema box office.

'Hello love, here again?' she would say. 'Here's your free tickets. Who are you bringing this time?'

After a few attempts we abandoned the sham altogether.

The reality was that our boyfriend was always delighted to get in for free. These were teenagers, and the only income they had was from pocket money or perhaps a paper round. The fact that they didn't have to pay was a great result.

This wasn't the only time Ma's advice about money caused me embarrassment. Against my better judgement, I heeded it once more when Steve from youth club invited me to Cricket St Thomas wildlife park. He looked at me as I stood with purse firmly closed, while he paid the entrance fee for just himself.

'All boys expect to pay on the first date,' Ma's words repeated in my ear. I stood firm, as a medieval maiden protecting the dignity of her knight. Even when both Steve and now the woman selling the tickets looked enquiringly at me, I held firm.

'Lucinda,' Steve said, 'it's one pound fifty to get in. You coming or what?'

On days when it was just Caroline and me, we would head off down the street or go up to the park. It felt as though the whole town was our garden. We had the freedom to go where we wanted. There was the Victorian park with its elaborate bandstand, a surprise sanctum amongst the open air paths. And we could wander into any of the shops. W.H. Smith, to look at the LPs and stationery, was our favourite.

In the late summer, with the shop now closed on Sundays, we would head off to the beach at Durdle Door or Bowleaze Cove for a long family walk. If it started to rain or get cold, Pa would reach inside his anorak pocket and pull out a crumpled bag of sweets. Sucking on wine gums under cover of a tree when you would really rather be at home was the comforting boost we needed. Sometimes we would be cut off by the tide or find our path blocked by high cliffs. With Ma starting to panic, Pa would grab our hands and swing us up one by one over the rocks. There was never a ledge he couldn't swing us over, no matter the height. Even when daylight began to fade and the bats started swirling in the air, you knew with him we would always find our way home.

Pa seemed fearless of physical danger. Whenever we went on holiday to the coast, down to Cornwall, he used to swim quite far out to sea. Responding to Ma's concerned calls of 'Can you see him?' we would sit up from our sunbathing to look for him and usually make him out as a bobbing head, the furthest swimmer out at sea. We would all feel relieved when he started swimming back to shore, and came back onto the beach, crashing out glistening onto his beach towel.

Sometimes we would drive out to the pretty villages of

Bockhampton or Stinsford, near Kingston Maurward. Ma would point out the catkins and hedgerow flowers as we walked along the riverside path eating beech nuts off the ground. Sometimes we would get waylaid in Stinsford churchyard, looking out for the grave where Thomas Hardy's heart is buried. We would do our best to read the fading inscriptions on the gravestones, some covered in moss or aged beyond legibility. Some graves were neglected, without sign of having being visited in years, others had fresh or just fading flowers. If we came across a grave with artificial flowers, Ma would become agitated, making us promise never to put plastic flowers on her grave. I feel the same. There is something gaudily garish about that, it just looks wrong.

15

A Brutal Education

BOTH MY PARENTS recognised that a good education could set you up for life and they wanted to give us this advantage as best they could. Ma felt her schooling at St Margaret's in Bristol had given her a solid grounding and laid the foundation for her nursing career. Although Pa's education had been disrupted by the war, he later studied for his Higher National Diploma at night school, completing assignments at the kitchen table after work.

Moving from Weymouth to Dorchester to take on the shop meant that my sister and I had to move schools. My parents thought that as they would be working all hours, with little time to help us with reading and homework, they should send us to the more intensive local prep school. The primary school in Weymouth had been a gentle affair. I remember the field of bluebells just off the playground where I stood mesmerised one day. There is something about that shade of blue that feels so hopeful and nostalgic, even for a six year old. I used to love coming home with my story book and reading it to Pa, sitting on his knee in the lounge at Tiffany's, the heady combination of love and learning, the one feeding off the other. The nurturing gifts of time and encouragement are the most valuable of all to the novice scholar.

Dorchester Preparatory School, run by the formidable Mrs Pellow, was to be a less sympathetic experience, humiliation and fear being her main teaching styles. I think she lured parents in with the dual promises of discipline and getting pupils into the grammar school. But there was a high price to pay. At every corner criticism and rebuke loomed.

The school itself was a double-fronted Victorian building, three storeys high with a basement. Its pebbledash exterior was painted from time to time, at one point becoming more tangerine than terracotta. The house sat on a steep lawn so that you had to crick your neck to look up at it from the pavement. The entrance, a heavy wooden door, was approached via steep steps, and its narrow path bordered by rose bushes that snared my thin cotton dress on windy days.

There was a concreted-over garden at the rear surrounded by raised flowerbeds, where the girls used to play elastics and cat's cradle or show off their stamp collections. I used to love my stamps, especially the ones with brightly coloured tropical fish from Bermuda or Australia. We lived in hope of finding a Penny Black or, at the very least, a good swap to complete a set. The playground was segregated, the boys nearest the school and the girls nearer the back, the boys being constantly shouted at to make sure their footballs didn't decapitate the dahlias.

Arriving mid-term, I found the other kids standoffish; their established friendships felt hard to break into. I was a stranger. Everything had changed for me. Not only my school and classmates, but my home, my home town and my parents' jobs. The same went for my sister. For a while it felt like we were castoffs: we had left the family home we knew and hadn't yet worked out in our own minds our new sense of identity or position in the world. Fortunately we had each other, the strength that comes from cohesiveness.

Whereas the teachers at my primary school were uniformly kind, several of the teachers at Dorchester prep were much more antagonistic. With hindsight, I can see that the headmistress was sadistic. Mrs Pellow had started the school in the 1950s, evidently not from the yearnings of an altruistic heart.

She wore the county uniform of cream blouses and long knitted cardigans with pockets that she sank her hands deep into when she walked. Her large pendulous breasts lay unpronounced beneath the loosely woven fabric. Waves of grey-blonde hair would fall across her eyes mid-reprimand and get pinned back forcibly as if she were grabbing the arm of a disobedient child. Tweed skirts revealed thick calves, and misshapen feet in frumpy shoes contributed to the slight tilt in her gait.

She used to sit in the front corner of the classroom near the sash window on a slightly raised wooden chair, playing with her glasses, swinging them round and round by the curved part that normally hooked over her ear. The more annoyed she became, the slower the spin of the glasses in her hand. If you hesitated too long with your answer, she would stop spinning her glasses altogether and take the curved end into her mouth and chew on it, exposing her teeth.

She would ask you a question with her face muscles taut, squeezed into a strained smile of expectation, stretching her pursed lips, her eyes half-closed as she peered down the trajectory of her nose. It was a frightening ordeal for any seven year old and made recollection of the right answer, or any answer, virtually impossible. Like a fly caught in a web you knew when you were trapped. Abstention from answering brought no relief. Her response to an ignorant silence brought forth a spitting boom of a voice.

'Speak up!' she would bellow, which had the opposite effect, causing my mouth to dry so that when I did speak, all I could manage was a whisper. In this state of fear I could barely remember my own name. I wasn't the only one to be treated this way. She might have had some favourites but even they were not guaranteed protection. Humiliation was her game.

The worst moments came when you had to line up next to her to have your homework marked, moving forward one by one, anticipating the worst. One time, as I proffered my open exercise book and my father's fountain pen with which to mark it, she yanked both from my hands. With a flourish of her right hand she drew a diagonal line across the page starting at the bottom left corner, and letting go of the pen at its furthest point. The pen took off like a missile flying above the heads of the seated pupils, crash-landing under one of the desks. The exercise book, meanwhile, was on a similar course, having been skimmed like a stone into the classroom mêlée with a flick of her hand.

None of my seated classmates moved. No one looked up or seemed to notice. No one seemed to think that this was in the slightest bit odd. No foot slid sideways to scoop up the pen or the book to push them forward into the alleyway between the desks. No one helped. Everyone just carried on with their work, heads down, fearful of further flying objects.

I bent down on my hands and knees amongst the pencil shavings and torn-off fingernail crescents, eraser rubbings and strands of hair, to search beneath the rows of lidded desks. I found the nib first, by someone's shoe, and then I had to crawl around and find the barrel and the lid. Bending down on all fours, the dusty film on my palms, I was careful not to expose my pants in my short 1970s dress, disoriented, trying to match feet to faces from a subterranean map. There was no time for tears; I was on a mission. She might throw my pen across the room without a care for me or it, but I was the one who was going to have to go back to Pa and explain what had happened.

I had a run of arriving at school to be told to go down to the basement to the remedial class. Although it had the benefit of getting you away from Mrs Pellow, it had the disadvantage that you had to catch up what you had missed and so I fell further behind. Funny how the word remedial comes from the word remedy, and in a way it was. At least it gave me a breathing space away from the dragon, a chance to learn without fear. But it did feel embarrassing and unsettling not to know where you would be, from one day to the next.

Mrs Pellow could turn up at any time anywhere in the school, like a ghost, apparently able to walk through walls. She seemed to have mastered the dimension of time travel, which added to her mystery. You might have the misfortune to encounter her at the bottom of the stairs on the ground floor of the tiled hallway, just after coming in through the front door. And then, just when you thought the coast was clear, there she would appear again on the upstairs landing. How did she manage that? It must have been a building of secret passageways and back staircases.

There was no privacy, so humiliation was a public spectacle. Even in the toilets, there were no doors to separate the cubicles, just a stained curtain that didn't get laundered. The fear of being interrupted was very real. I used to noisily scrape my shoe on the floor to make it known that the cubicle was busy.

There was a church nearby that I could see from the rear classroom window. Each St George's Day it used to fly the red and white flag from its flagpole. I used to wonder where it was. It was only years later it became obvious. It was St George's church in Fordington, where my parents had got married, the same church you can see as you approach Dorchester from Grey's Bridge. I lost my bearings at that school. I felt cut off and unable to make sense of things. I wasn't thriving, I was failing. School photographs show a child I barely recognise with an anxious gaze and cracked lips. Even my hair looks stressed.

The lunchtime bell portended little by way of excitement. There were no delicious treats to look forward to, no cheery dinner ladies serving ample helpings of sugary puddings. We suffered joyless food, prepared without heart. Oh to have had lunches cooked by my darling Great-Aunt Winnie, who had been a dinner lady for many years. She would have looked after us. There would have been no burnt toad in the hole or cold rice pudding for us. We would have had Cornish pasties to eat out of our hands, or proper roasts with puffed-up crispy Yorkshires. When I complained one day about the hairy green caterpillar in my salad I was met with cutting sarcasm. 'Aren't you lucky!' came the response as Mrs Bowen's fat fingers pinched it off its lettuce leaf bed. We used to joke that the headmistress dined on caviar and roast chicken like a queen in her flat upstairs.

A few of the teachers seemed not to fit the mould and were my salvation. One of them was my English teacher, Mr Wilde, a skeletal man in tweed trousers with heavy turn-ups whose wiry frame jutted out from beneath his formal clothes. He seemed ancient but not out of touch. He was the relief to monotonous put downs and dents in my self-confidence.

I felt a special connection with him, enjoying his dry wit and rants against Enid Blyton – 'that dreadful woman'. I loved his irreverence. He would stand tall at the front of the class, one hand balancing an open book, the other hanging casually from his trouser pocket. Reading aloud from *Emil and the Detectives*, he would pause to ask a question, eyebrows raised above his horn-rimmed glasses. I would catch the smile in his eyes which seemed aimed only at me. He led me through the adventures of *The Silver Sword*, *Charlotte's Web* and *The Lion, the Witch and the Wardrobe* to a land where I was untouchable. Wherever you are now, Mr Wilde, I hope the reading material is good.

My other escapism came in the form of our ballet teacher, Miss Hornbeam. Dark haired and sylphlike, she was poised and graceful with theatrically elongated neck and hands. She stood deliberately in her black footless tights and ballet pumps wearing the wrap-around cardigan I coveted. She was less teacher, more artist, transforming the soulless basement room into a bustling theatre set with words alone.

'Today, girls, we are doing *Coppélia*.' Sweeping her arms gracefully to point her directions, she invited us to, 'Imagine the opening scene of a town festival. Let's have market stalls down here and little shops selling fruit and vegetables, handmade toys and homemade sweets. Let's have streamers from the buildings and a band playing a march over in this corner.'

We were transformed by this fairy godmother into ballerinas. Under her command we had ditched our grey uniforms and brown buckled shoes for tulle tutus with brocade corsets. We became the corps de ballet in pink satin ballet shoes with criss-crossed ribbons around our ankles. 'Keep your eyes front, girls, look out from the stage,' she would say as we pliéd or chasséd about the room.

Although we danced in a dingy basement that just hours before had served us cabbage and cold custard, under her guidance we were enraptured by her spell as surely as if she had waved a magic wand. It was a place without fear where all that concerned us was the point of our toes and the shape of our hands. When class finished it was like being woken from a dream you weren't quite ready to leave. I would hang on to it for as long as I could. Then I would trudge back to the classroom, like Cinderella returning to her miserable life once the magic spell had been broken.

Later, as the Eleven Plus loomed, ballet and English lessons with stories gave way to the doldrums of practice papers. Our imaginative, rebellious Mr Wilde was replaced by a diminutive teacher, called Mrs Weisman, private, reserved and quietly spoken. She didn't have much fun to share, being charged with instructing us in verbal reasoning drill and the duller points of grammar.

But my class were all astounded when Mrs Pellow barged into our English lesson one day. She marched in and took her position at the front of the room, next to a surprised Mrs Weisman, and announced without preamble, 'Now don't be alarmed that your teacher's handwriting is so small. The reason for this, children, is because she was a prisoner in a Nazi concentration camp as a child and has been traumatised by the experience.'

I remember staring open-mouthed at this strange and sudden revelation. Mrs Weisman adopted a look we all recognised, complete humiliation, her eyes drilling the floor to swallow her up. Clearly this was an intimate detail she was not yet ready to share. Mrs Pellow exited as swiftly as she had entered, leaving us confused about the purpose of her announcement. I realised then that it isn't just children who get bullied.

While I was at that school I won a national art competition, sponsored by Dairylea. My painting was of a large brown cow in a field with a clover flower in its mouth. Ma had taught me how to draw fields as sweeping arcs of rounded hills rather than as straight lines, which, I was later told, is what the judges had particularly liked. The painting became part of Dairylea's national marketing campaign for its cheese, appearing on billboards around the country. One of my friends had her picture taken standing in front of it somewhere in London.

My prize was forty pounds, and Pa came with me to the jewellers in Hardye Arcade to help me choose a watch. It was brilliant having a grown-up amount of money to spend. I picked out one with a gold face and a fine navy blue calfskin strap. I wore it proudly for years.

Despite winning, I hadn't realised until recently that I've never thought of myself as being particularly gifted at art. The art teacher at Dorchester prep was a miserable soul incapable of encouragement or praise. The most ingrained lesson that I learned about art from her was that I wasn't very good at it. Even in the term I won the national art competition, my art report reads, 'Has worked with interest and shown much ability in her picture making.' It was the same thing she wrote every year.

My school reports are compiled in a green A5 booklet embossed with the name of the school in gold lettering. As I read through them I feel disconnected, believing they must be about another child. The headmistress's comments seem written about a girl who wasn't me. Comments like, 'A term of happy effort and happy progress. Well done, Lucinda!' and, 'She loves doing her best at school. Good for Lucinda!' These are words written in a theatrically dramatic hand, the letters strung together by long flowing loops, suggesting she was singing as she wrote. There is no reference to the pen and book flinging incident.

I had felt unable to do anything about my unhappiness there. It was only years later at a school reunion that I bumped into one of my old classmates, Susan. I had forgotten that she had left after only one year. She told me that she had had such a hideous time there that she pleaded with her parents to take her away. She left and went to a different school where she was very happy. It never dawned on me that that was an option. I never thought for a moment that I could get out of the situation, that I could go home and tell my parents that I wanted to leave. I accepted it for what it was. I assumed that they knew what was going on, that this was just part of education. Susan and I also spoke about the Mrs Weisman incident, which she remembered as vividly as me.

I felt so lucky to return home each night to a sense of normality. Meeting us after school to walk home along the tree-lined avenue of South Walks, Pa would invariably produce a wrapped sweet from his anorak pocket. In autumn stooping to pick up conkers or scuffing up piles of horse chestnut leaves, we would chomp and chatter through a mouthful of chocolate eclairs.

Unlike me at school, both of my parents were good at

standing up for themselves. Ma refused to be pushed around by the reps who would come into the shop to try to sell their latest collection of gifts or cards. They would stand at the front till with their heavy plastic display folders, insisting that she take a minimum order costing hundreds of pounds and at least one of every style of card.

'Look,' she would say, 'we are not W.H. Smith's, we are Osmond's. That is not how we do things here.' So, the reps would either have to agree to her handpicked selection or leave without making a sale. As time went on and the shop became more successful, she had even more clout, and she exercised it. Pa didn't allow himself to get pushed around either. On one occasion, when he was repeatedly being presented with an invoice he disputed, he took a red felt tip pen and wrote the word 'BALLS' across it in capital letters. He sent it back and never heard another word.

16

Love & Youth

'THERE'S NO NIGHT life in this town! There are no discos, the pubs won't serve us and the nearest ice rink is an hour away.' Such were the gripes of the young people of the town. For the teenager, Dorchester at night seemed to have very little to offer. The youth-club discos in the Methodist Hall were unlikely to be a fruitful search. Being propositioned by a spiky-haired, pogoing punk was hardly going to lead to the sort of relationships we were after.

As a teenager, Pa had taken dance lessons to help him meet girls. I admired his forethought. He knew girls liked to dance so he decided that he had better get good at it. He was an adept mover on the floor and always keen to get up and dance with Ma when the occasion arose. He certainly wasn't one of those men who would slouch off to the bar when the band struck up and leave their wives toe-tappingly desperate for a dance partner. Pa was up there, doing his version of the twist, moving his hips and not taking himself too seriously.

My parents met at a dance, as people used to do. It was one of those chance encounters that should not have happened. Pa was never meant to have been there, he should have been hundreds of miles away in Spain. A sudden bout of appendicitis had done for him, and scuppered his planned holiday of driving a couple of friends down to the Costa del Sol. The holiday had to be abandoned as he was the only one with a car.

Instead of partying in Benidorm he went to recuperate with his cousin Bob in Bournemouth. On the night in question, he had recovered enough to make an appearance at The Royal Ballrooms, Boscombe, an elegant affair in its day with wide sweeping stairways leading down Fred Astaire style to the huge dance floor. Here the first buds of love bloomed for both Pa and Bob who, like in a Hollywood film, fell for the pair of pretty, dark-eyed girls chatting at the bar. Ma and her nursing friend Mary were enjoying some downtime away from the wards. It wasn't quite a double wedding, but close enough.

If Pa hadn't been taken ill, he would never have met Ma. If he hadn't taken those dance lessons, perhaps he wouldn't have impressed her.

A long distance relationship proved workable. Ma was working as a nurse in Bournemouth, as was Mary, and Pa worked as an engineer in Kent. He and Bob used to pile into Pa's Rochdale and drive the 120 miles to Bournemouth in time to pick up the girls from their shift, stopping off en route at the Hogs Back Hotel to change drivers.

For us, meeting boys at discos wasn't ideal. It might have been fine in Ma and Pa's day, but for us, those dark, loud territories weren't the best places to start a relationship. What we needed was for the boys to come to us. And to that end, the shop proved an invaluable stage.

Here, boys were on our turf. It was a safe place to be, standing in the sweet shop with Pa who would always be ready to disappear off down to the cellar if he sensed I needed a bit of space to talk. 'I'm just going to get some more paper bags, Lucinda. Back in a minute,' he would say with a wink, or he would walk away, straightening the jars in the passageway. If I was working in the card shop, any boy would be under the watchful gaze of Ma or Julie, a vetting committee who didn't miss much. You could be sure that Julie would keep you abreast of any unfavourable gossip about him, his family or their comings and goings in the town. Somehow she would have the inside knowledge on the boys to avoid, titbits of which even the *Dorset Echo* wasn't aware. 'He's been to borstal,' or 'his mother was done for shoplifting the other week' were the type of comments that gave us the heads up on the characteristics of our customers. 'Never!' was Ma's usual reply. 'I don't know how you know this stuff, Julie.'

One lad told Caroline afterwards that he had come into the shop so many times but had never been able to pluck up the courage to ask her out. He ended up buying tens of birthday cards because he felt he couldn't leave empty handed. If there was someone special we had our eye on, Julie would conspire to set up a meeting, developing a special code. She would come through to the sweet shop to find me and I would hastily excuse myself.

'Quick! Go and tidy the cards. That boy you like has gone up the end of the shop looking for you,' she would say.

'I'll just be a minute, Pa. I've got to help Julie with something,' I would reply, as Pa shot me a bemused look as he carried on serving a customer, accepting the ruse without question.

The end of the card shop was L-shaped and I would usually find the boy wandering about there. It was perfect, and so much less intimidating as I could talk to him while I straightened the birthday cards, reuniting them with strayed envelopes. If the conversation went on longer and there was no more tidying to do, I could pull open the large drawer underneath the card shelves and pull out a wad of new cards to display. The options for extending the conversation were endless. The only problem, of course, was that it wasn't very private. It was like being chaperoned by a shopful of customers. Sometimes it felt as though customers were crowding in and lingering a little longer than necessary.

And so it turned out that the shop made the often embarrassing situation of meeting boys much easier. For us, it was perfect, even if for the boys it was sometimes a little confusing. Caroline's old boyfriend Tim recalls their first encounter.

'One late summer's afternoon as I was wandering along South Street, I noticed a girl in a yellow dress walking ahead of me. The dress had criss-cross straps revealing a beautiful back, toned and tanned. As she walked, the tip of her ponytail bounced off the nape of her neck. She stood out from the normal summer crowd. I didn't know who she was, but something inside me screamed, "I need to know!"

'I followed her up the street, dodging the stream of people in my way, keeping my eyes pinned on her yellow dress. Suddenly she took a left turn, disappearing into a shop. Without thinking, I dashed out of the crowd to follow her. I found myself in a small shop so it should have been easy to find her. I looked left and right but couldn't find her anywhere, she had vanished into thin air. In a panic I suddenly realised that I must have appeared a bit strange, so I picked up a random card and went to the till to pay. I was served by a tall man with a well-trimmed beard, who looked at me bemusedly as he gave me my change.

'Drifting back out onto the street I headed for home, still trying to solve the mystery in my head. Where had she gone? Then it came to me. Perhaps she worked there. Perhaps she had gone upstairs. I made up my mind to phone the shop as soon as I got home. Finding the number in the phone book and with a racing heart I called the shop to try and track her down.'

Pa (the man with the well-trimmed beard) answered and connected Tim and Caroline, the result of a search in the Yellow Pages for the girl in the yellow dress.

Sometimes, though, the familiarity with customers was less welcome. An anonymous Valentine's card raised my hopes and created suspense and mystery around it. But it turned out not to be sent from any desired admirer. Instead I learned that it was from one of the old men who I used to serve roll-up tobacco. He was about sixty years older than me, or that's what I thought at the time. Finding out the truth was worse than not receiving the card in the first place. Valentine's cards sent in jest can be dangerous, though it didn't have as devastating an effect on me as it did for poor Bathsheba and Mr Boldwood, her unrequited lover in Hardy's *Far from the Madding Crowd*. But, it made me realise how vulnerable our hearts can be when we imagine the possibility of love in the air. We let down our guard and ready ourselves to receive that affection when in fact it may not be forthcoming, nor, on closer inspection, desired. For Bathsheba, her playful prank backfired, she never intended to be found out. She unwittingly opened up a chapter that was to haunt her for the rest of Boldwood's life, and she learned the hard way not to trifle with matters of the heart. An anonymous promise of affection to someone in search of love cannot fail but hurt when they realise it is not the real thing.

I don't think Pa faced such trials, love and youth for him were less complicated. He was fortunate to be a teenager at the birth of youth culture, the same generation as Elvis Presley, John Lennon and Mick Jagger. He used to speak excitedly about the time he went to see Bill Haley and the Comets; he had never seen anything like it. I think it was a turning point for him, his eyes widening to what the world had to offer. Pa had dabbled with the fashions, blaming his skinny feet on the winklepicker shoes he used to wear. We too styled ourselves on the bands of the day, from glossy *Smash Hits* and the burgeoning music videos that began to replace the mimed performances on *Top of the Pops*. Dorchester may have lacked the dynamic scene of London or Liverpool, yet we were as eager to play with the trends as young people there were. Youth culture overflowed into our lives as much as it did for urban teenagers. We had our punks with their dyed spiked hair with chains across their legs, and our Mods, neat and sharp in black and white. We had our Siouxsie Sioux and Blondie lookalikes in dark eye make-up and peroxide hair. My allegiance was to the New Romantics, all frilled shirts and floppy hair, where even the boys had black kohled eyes. But no one except sailors had tattoos back then, not professionally done anyway. The only ones around were DIY jobs, made with a school compass and a cartridge pen.

Ma ragged Caroline's hair like the fun-loving, dungaree-wearing trio of Bananarama, which was not that different from the rags Ma used to wear as a child before bed. The most labour-intensive style to maintain was the Victorian nightdress and knickerbockers we wore, sourced from local antique fairs. These were drawn threadwork undergarments that would have been sewn by candlelight, items best suited to a young Victorian woman's trousseau, now being worn defiantly down the street in broad daylight. Ma embraced our fashion choices with enthusiasm and didn't object to the kitchen looking like a professional laundry, keeping our cottons as steamed and starched as a Ritz tablecloth.

We felt creative and strangely not in the least self-conscious. I am not sure I would be able to meet my Victorian petticoat-and-bloomers-wearing self today without a little eyebrow raising. Perhaps that's one of the benefits of youth – eccentricity comes with the territory.

17

Crate Sex

ONE OF THE problems with taking over an existing business was that Ma and Pa had to learn the ropes fast. Mr and Mrs Walker, the previous proprietors, had agreed to stay on and run the shop with them for the first fortnight. But after a week, despite still not knowing exactly what they were doing, they bid the Walkers thanks and farewell. The shop wasn't big enough for all of them and they could do without customers being greeted with the line, 'Yes, it will be different! Give them time. They'll learn it!' They had had enough of feeling like novices and wanted to get on and do it their way. 'Come on, Jude, we can do this on our own,' Pa said.

After the first six months they soon realised which of the products weren't worth their while. One of these was fresh milk. The difficulty with making the decision to stop selling milk was that it was seen as part of a service, and that they might lose customers as a result. It is quite amazing to think of the vast array of places you can go now to buy a pint of milk, but when we took over the business, many people in the town were still reliant on coming to a sweet shop to buy their pinta.

Selling milk generated some quite interesting characters.

One particular woman used to shove open the door so hard it would make the glass shudder. She would stand at the entrance to the shop waving her walking stick in the air to attract attention, shouting, 'I say! I'd like a pint of milk and ten Benson & Hedges.' Pa and I would fire a quick glance at each other in acknowledgement, before one of us stepped out into the street to serve her. If there were customers in the shop, heads would turn and brows would frown in unison. Once we had served her, she would pack the milk and cigarettes into her tartan shopping trolley before padding off down the street in her moccasin slippers.

The milk would be delivered early each morning. We had two red milk crates that held about twenty bottles each, positioned outside the shop, just in front of the confectionery window. There was a lot of wastage. Some bottles were pilfered, some bottles got dropped and smashed, and in summer, the birds would peck at the silver foil lids and spoil the milk. Often we barely broke even, the mark-up on a 12½p pint of milk being just ½p.

Some mornings Pa would be annoyed to find a stream of dog urine dribbling down the side of the bottles. He would then have to discard the milk and soapsud the pavement before opening up the shop.

But the final straw came one night when we were still living in the flat above. We returned late one night after having had dinner out with family, and parked outside the shop. As Pa went to unlock the sweet shop door, he saw a couple having sex on the empty milk crates.

'Do you mind! I've got children with me,' Pa said.

'Give us a minute, I'm not done yet!' replied the man.

'Get off my crates. Now!' Pa replied as the couple reluctantly disentangled themselves and disappeared off down the street.

'Right, that's it! The milk is going,' Pa announced, relieved at finally being able to justify getting rid of the stuff.

It was generally the older customers who felt the inconvenience of us stopping selling milk.

'Why don't you sell milk any more, Mr Osmond?'

'Ah yes, Mrs White, well, that's quite a story,' he replied, as he reached for the broom to sweep up some imaginary sugar dust off the floor.

18

Chewing Gum Chase

O N THE WALL outside the shop next to the Plaza cinema hoarding was something else that we had inherited – a Wrigley's Spearmint chewing gum dispenser. The gum machine, though a source of some income, was also a source of irritation. Quite often it was my job to refill it, which was a cumbersome exercise. I would collect together the rickety fold-out stool, a brand new box of chewing gum, a container for collecting the coins, and, not forgetting the key, carry them all out into the street. Unlocking the front casing and climbing up onto the stool, I would pull off the heavy metal cover and gently lower it to the ground, counter-levering it against my weight. I didn't enjoy this job as the cover was very heavy and you had to be quite a contortionist to lift the cover back onto the machine, trying hard all the time not to fall off the stool, which had a tendency to wobble sideways. The added complication was that you couldn't leave the machine open because of the risk of theft. If you had forgotten something, you had to close up the machine, go back into the shop, then come back outside and repeat the procedure all over again. At least the rickety stool would still be there when you returned; no one would want to run off with that.

It was always startling to witness the ingenuity of people, to see what had been passed off as coins. We would find old ones, foreign ones and at least a button or two. We would collect up the array of coins, real and counterfeit, and replenish the stock, filling the machine with chewing gum, stacking the little white shiny packets of gum one on top of the other.

One Saturday, to my relief, Pa said that he would fill the machine, so I stayed inside and looked after the shop. However, he had under-calculated how many packets of chewing gum he needed, so he left the cover off for a moment while he popped back in to collect more.

Pa then got delayed serving a customer. Suddenly we noticed the shop assistant across the road at Bollom, the dry cleaners, pointing and waving at us. She was a very large woman with a weakness for our chocolate raisins. To begin with Pa thought she was just being friendly so we waved back. Then it dawned on us.

'I think she's pointing at something outside, Pa,' I said.

'The gum machine!' he said as he sprinted out of the shop.

To his horror, he found it completely empty. Looking around for where the gum could have gone, he caught sight of a lad running off down the road, leaving a trail of foil wrappers behind him. Pa legged it after him, catching up with him outside Frisby's. He grabbed hold of the culprit by the scruff of the neck and dragged him back to the shop where he started interrogating him. The boy could hardly deny his crime, his pockets and mouth being full of chewing gum. Spitting it out he readied himself to start answering Pa's questions.

'Right, sonny, what's your name?'

'David Cassidy.'

'Where do you live?'

'Emmerdale Farm.'

'Right. Don't you ever come in my shop again, do you hear? Any more trouble from you and I'll be round to speak to your dad.'

Sensing the interrogation was over, the lad got up, pulled his Parka hood over his head, and sidled back out into the street.

'Well,' Pa said, 'what do you make of that?' as he looked down at the details he had jotted on the back of a paper bag.

'Pa, I don't think that's his real name. I think he's made it all up.'

'What do you mean?'

'Well, David Cassidy is a pop star and *Emmerdale Farm* is a programme on TV. Grandma watches it.'

'Would you believe it!' Pa said in exasperation, looking as if he had lost all sense of the world. If we were an off-licence I think he would have broken open the brandy.

I used to see the boy around town occasionally but he never again came into the shop. The tale was retold many times, on each occasion Pa's disbelief and indignation at the blatant lies never lessening in their intensity. Not long after, like the milk bottles, the chewing gum machine met its demise.

19

Not So Sweet

WE WILL NEVER know how much stock we lost through theft. Once we had the expanded shop we would watch any suspicious-looking people, Ma even confronting them, saying, 'I'm watching you!' Occasionally I would get a wink or a sign from her to keep an eye on someone. The drill was to follow them around the shop until they realised they were being watched and they left to try their luck elsewhere. It was only years later that we discovered one of the temporary staff had been stealing tobacco every week for her father, seeing it as a perk of the job rather than an act of theft.

Things took a dramatic turn one Monday evening when Ma was working in the sweet shop. Pa was at home, working on the car, repairing a faulty seatbelt. I had taken him a cup of tea and seen that he was winding the seatbelt around the pre-tensioner very carefully, making sure that the tension was even all the way round. He had been at it for hours, and was pleased to have nearly wound it up fully, so that he could fit it back into the car.

'This is a job I won't want to repeat!' he said as he eyed the oatmeal biscuit. 'Nearly done!'

Just then, the phone rang.

It was Ma. I knew from her voice that something was wrong. Through what sounded like clenched teeth she said, 'Could you ask Daddy to come to the phone quickly?' I went out to get him. He had nearly finished, but I could see that if he let go of the seatbelt webbing, the whole thing would unravel and he would have to start again.

'Tell her I can't come now!' Pa said. 'I'll call her back when I've finished.'

I repeated the message to Ma, anticipating that this wouldn't suffice. With a deep intake of breath she said more sharply, 'Tell him something's happened at the shop. I need to speak to him straight away.'

Pa got up from the ground, not pleased to have his work interrupted. He let go of the wound-up webbing and it unravelled like a freed snake.

'What is it you want, Judith?'

I couldn't hear her reply, only his response: 'I'll be there in two minutes!'

Caroline and I were bundled into the car. We didn't even have time to change out of our slippers. Pa drove us as fast as he could to the shop. It was a good ten minutes' drive, but I think he did it quicker than that.

It was a shock to see Ma with her mouth and eye badly swollen. She looked shaken, like she had been knocked out of her body. There was a policeman with her who I recognised from his regular visits to buy Murray Mints. Ma was telling him what had happened.

'A man came in earlier this afternoon, I'd never seen him before. He came over to me, looking around the shop all the time. Then he looked straight at me and asked for a box of matches. He was wearing army clothes and I thought to myself, "He's a big strong bloke."

'We'd had a really busy day and there was a lot of cash in the till. I'd been here with one of our staff, but she went home at about five o'clock. The man came back in again just after she'd left, when the shop was empty and I was on my own. I'd been stocking up the cigarettes when I turned round to find him right beside me. He went to pay for a bar of chocolate and as I pressed the button on the till to open it, I could feel his breath on my face. I knew he was going to hit me, he was so close to me. I looked up at him and he punched me in the mouth and up into my cheek. He took some notes out of the till and disappeared. I pulled myself up by hanging onto the open till drawer and ran out into the street shouting, "Stop thief! He's just robbed the till!" Maureen from the chemist next door came running out, and that's when she called the police.'

Roadblocks had been set up around Dorchester, the police presuming that the thief had come from Bovington Camp, the local army base. The police needed a photograph of Ma's injuries. The officer suggested, perhaps to comfort her or Caroline and me, to take one of the three of us together. It was a bizarre photograph, Ma in the middle with her black eye and swollen mouth, feeling beaten up and self-conscious, flanked by Caroline and me in our school uniforms. It was odd, not just because Ma had a distorted face, but because as children we were used to smiling when someone took a photograph of us. The expressions on our three faces show us looking at the camera not quite knowing what to do.

The thief was never found. Fortunately, he got away with very little. Not long before he had come back in the second time, Mrs Eyres had alerted Ma to the amount of notes in the till. This had prompted Ma to give them to her to put in the cash box upstairs in the office for safe keeping before she left for the day. All that was left in the till was the float, which, apart from the coins, was a few pound notes and a couple of fives.

The mugging at Osmond's made it into the *Dorset Echo* and was the talk of the town for days. Turnover the following week was exceptional as customers came in to show their support.

Roger Gould, who ran the department store across the road, had been locking up when he had heard the screech of brakes from Pa pulling up outside our shop.

'I've never seen Clive drive so quickly,' he said. 'I thought it was *The Sweeney*!'

Some customers came to stare, some to sympathise; some were really upset while others threatened violence themselves.

'If I knew who it was, Mrs Osmond, I'd show him my fist!' said Mr Foot, a pensioner from Puddletown.

The photograph has gone now, torn up by Ma years ago.

'We don't want that!' she said, as she ripped it in two. She didn't want a reminder of the day she was knocked down. 'We're the Osmonds. We're not having that.'

20

Snoops & Spies

P A USED TO say that the odds were stacked against small businesses; there were very few incentives or leg-ups from the government. The self-employed walked a balancing act between bank loans and rent reviews, tax man audits and making their own pension provision. The security for bank loans is often the family home. Being self-employed is not for the faint-hearted.

You had to be alert, totally on top of the figures, and it was lucky that he was. One day he noticed that we were overdrawn by sixty thousand pounds. He couldn't work it out, it stressed him for days. He challenged the bank but they said the account was correct. He went back over the figures with a fine comb and eventually found the cause – the bank had put the decimal point in the wrong place. There was no apology from the bank, no acknowledgement of their fault. It was a huge relief, but it was an episode that undermined his trust in financial institutions.

Our accountant, Harry Gill, was from Yorkshire. He used to come down to stay with us to prepare the accounts and always arrived bearing gifts, usually books. The best one was *The Hobbit*, still one of my favourites. I hadn't met any accountants until then, nor anyone from Yorkshire. We used to look forward to his visits, when he would entertain us at dinner with tales of dodgy tax deeds of trawler owners and fishermen from Hull. He would spread his arms wide to enliven his stories, a lit Benson & Hedges a permanent feature between his fingers; his charismatic smile and broad accent enhancing his tales.

Harry had received a letter from HM Inspector of Taxes that they were not satisfied with Pa's tax returns. Pa would have to attend a formal audit and be interviewed by the tax man. Pa was very worried, and as the day of the audit drew closer, he became even more anxious, asking Harry what he should say and what he thought was going to happen.

'Don't worry, Clive,' Harry said. 'Leave the talking to me. I'll answer all the questions.'

The tax man, however, had different ideas.

When they got into the small windowless room, the small humourless man said, 'Right, when I address my questions to Mr Gill, I expect Mr Gill to reply. When I address my questions to Mr Osmond, I expect Mr Osmond to reply. I do not want you to answer each other's questions. Are we clear?'

With the scene set, and not how they had rehearsed it, the tax man fired questions, made assumptions and generally interrogated Pa for an hour.

'You see, Mr Osmond, I come across a lot of people like you. My job doesn't have perks like yours and I make it my business to make sure that people like you aren't getting ahead of themselves, taking more than their dues. I'm here to make sure you play by the rules, like I have to.

'How many boxes of chocolates do you take for your wife in a year?' he asked.

'She doesn't eat chocolate. She would rather have perfume as a gift. Or a grapefruit,' Pa replied.

'How many cards does your wife take out the shop for family and friends? How many sweets do your kids take every week?' The questions kept coming, Pa surprised by their ferocity and the assumption that he was a liar. None of us used the shop as a private larder. There were never boxes of chocolates lying around at home. We ate the odd sweet when we were working in the shop, and if I was hungry after a netball match, I might pinch a few to keep me going. But if I wanted something like a bar of chocolate, I would pay for it, using my staff discount of course.

Finally the tax man unleashed what he thought was his greatest coup.

'Tell me about your yacht, the one you've got moored in Poole Harbour.'

'I don't own a boat!' Pa replied.

'We've seen you out sailing.'

'Yes, with my friend Stuart. It's his boat, not mine.'

At the end of the meeting the tax man presented his scenario for settlement. It was larger than Pa would have liked but less than he had feared.

When he came back to the shop with Harry, Pa looked grey.

'How did it go?' Ma asked.

'Don't ask!' Pa replied.

'You look as white as a sheet. What happened?'

'He was horrible. I never want to go through that again.'

'He sounds evil!' Ma replied as she heard more of the detail.

'Put it behind you now, Clive,' Harry said. 'At least he didn't find out about that contraband brandy you've got hidden down that cellar. Come on, let's have a drink.'

The walls had ears, the tax man had his spies. Someone had reported Pa for seeming to live a life beyond the reach of an ordinary shopkeeper. In small towns, everyone knows everyone else's business, or at least they think they do. People jump to conclusions, especially people who have never been self-employed, who think that every penny you take is profit. Pull up in a new car or buy a new house and people may assume you've bought it outright. No one thinks about the loan agreement or mortgage that funds it, or the sleepless nights that may result from it.

Ma and Pa weren't smugglers, they weren't even tax evaders, but that's what the insinuation had been. The encounter fortified our family sense of unity. We had been challenged but emerged unscathed. The irony of it all was that it didn't encourage you to play by the rules; it made you want to bend them.

And so life went on and we navigated the ups and downs that came our way. And then something larger loomed on the horizon. For the most part, while we had the card shop, there was very little direct competition. WH Smith or the newsagent had a small greeting cards selection but nothing like our extensive offering. There were no other independent card shops. We were the first in the town.

But then a shop opposite us became vacant. It is always interesting to witness the hiatus between an empty shop and opening day to see what is to emerge. We soon found out that a new card shop was arriving on the scene. 'How dare they!' was our overriding response. We were united in disdain. We studied it warily as the frontage appeared and the display units went in. Their staff must have come in to us to do some snooping without us noticing. Julie went in for a look around, bold as brass, head held high, not in the least bit hiding what she was doing. I never went in there and certainly never Ma or Pa.

'They're not like us, Mrs Osmond,' was her report. 'It's boring, not like in here.'

It was a chain, everything ordered by head office, not handpicked or selected by someone who worked there. In fact, in terms of competition, it had little bearing on our trade. People are curious about new arrivals, they like to try something new. During the first few days of its opening, customers went in to have a look. But they came back to us, often with their own reports.

'Competition is good, it keeps you on your toes,' Ma would say. 'We'll ride above it.'

After the initial period of curiosity, the opening of the new card shop opposite didn't affect us at all. We just concentrated on what we had done before. There was no need for any knee-jerk reaction to do things differently – that would have been a disaster. Customers continued to come to us because they liked the personal service, because we knew them all by name.

Sometimes you would catch other traders in the town coming in to us, to see what competition we posed. There could be an overlap in the suppliers at the various trade shows we all attended. A celebratory wedding anniversary plate that we might take could also be bought by a shop selling homewares.

One day Pa caught the manager of Gould's department store in the shop.

'What are you up to, Richard?'

'I just wanted to see if you'd bought the anniversary china.'

'Just ask me, I'll tell you,' Pa replied.

The owner of a gift shop in Hardye Arcade used to send his children in to look around. When you have watched customers browsing and buying for fifteen years, you can tell when people are snooping or spying.

21

Religious Instruction

T HE PRIVATE EDUCATION at Dorchester preparatory wasn't a huge success in my case because I didn't make the cut for the grammar school; sitting the Eleven Plus with a broken writing arm didn't help. I was the only one in the class not to get a place apart from the handful of boys and girls who were sitting the Common Entrance for boarding schools. My parents didn't want me to board and I certainly didn't want to either. They came up with an alternative. I could go to the convent, a private school a few hundred yards away from Dorchester prep and still within walking distance of the shop, run by an order of nuns called Les Filles de La Croix. Some pupils boarded but Caroline and I would be day girls. I arrived at my senior school battle-hardened, with the real sense that if I could survive Mrs Pellow, I could survive anything.

I had no experience of nuns until I went to the convent, apart of course from what I had learned about them from Sister Maria in *The Sound of Music*. My only other awareness also came from a film, the gruelling inner struggle of Sister Luke played by Audrey Hepburn in *The Nun's Story*. I had cried to the point of exhaustion watching that film.

Going to buy the convent uniform with Ma was quite

exciting; a nun in full habit fussed around us, disappearing off to a separate room to return with armfuls of shirts and sweaters. It wasn't quite as dramatic as Sister Luke giving up her civilian clothes in return for those of a cloistered novice. Unlike her I wasn't having to turn my back on my family and home. But it did feel like a chance for change. I was more than ready to move on to the next phase of my school life.

I liked the uniform although it felt a little eccentric: a tartan kilt and tie, cream shirt and jumper, beige socks and brown lace up shoes. In winter we accessorised with brown gloves and green velour hats, which in summer were swapped for white gloves and straw boaters smelling of popcorn. We pinned the silver school badge, a crucifix bearing the Les Filles de La Croix inscription, to the grosgrain ribbon of our hats. We all loved wearing our kilts, so comforting to be wrapped in swathes of woven fabric. I think wearing tartan is confidence boosting even for a non-Scot.

Arriving from Dorchester prep the greatest benefit was that I had started learning French. Despite Mrs Pellow's teaching methods, some of it had stuck. It was just as well given that the French teacher, Madame Wales as we called her, was quite a force. She reminded me of an independent and ungrateful cat. Presenting her with your homework, she would acknowledge it with a sideways sniff, then walk off with her nose in the air, deeming it beneath her.

Her stylishness set her apart from the other teachers. Her A-line skirts and blouses were feminine and her cardigans worn slung over the shoulders gave her an air of Parisienne chic. I liked her selection of chunky heeled patent shoes and her neatly coiffed bob. She was aloof and mesmerising. When she considered a question, she would purse her rouged lips while stroking a lock of her hair, drawing it outwards and backwards as if moving a heavy lock of Bardotesque curls. She had little time for patience or small talk and was definitely not out to befriend us, but she maintained and enriched my enthusiasm for French for which I am grateful. She used to drive an old red Mini somewhat erratically. We would hear it racing up the drive, before coming to an abrupt halt in her usual parking space in front of the Gothic school.

English had always been my favourite subject. When I first arrived at the convent I was taught by Sister Maria Agretti. She was what I thought nuns would be like, sweet and gentle, meek and mild. Sister was smiling and encouraging and I soon found myself wanting to do well with her, in our study of *The Wind in the Willows*. Sadly, after the first term she was transferred to a convent in Devon and I never saw her again.

English lessons seemed designed for summer days. Stuck into a good book, taking it in turns to read a passage aloud, the gentle hum of the lawnmower drifting in through the open sash windows with my chin cradled warmly in my hand; shirt sleeves rolled up, socks pulled down, school satisfaction level at nine out of ten. It would have merited full marks if we could have had the lesson outdoors on the lawn.

There was no sixth form. Everyone left the convent by sixteen. It was not a place of aspiration where you could dream of exciting careers, of making your mark on the world. Right to the end of our time there, the nuns held out hope that we would follow them into taking holy orders. Even the 'non-Catholics' were expected to see the light and adopt the true religion. You could be confronted by a nun about your religious views anywhere, anytime. It was not uncommon for us 'nons' to be escorted into the boarders' bathroom, and with the door locked behind us, be told that it really was time we became Catholic and asked when we were going to convert.

In chapel one particularly hot day, kneeling at the pews, heads bowed with our eyes closed as Sister Eugene led the prayers, one of the girls passed out with a thud on the floor. We looked up startled to see who it was and saw her out cold on the carpet. Sister seemed reluctant to make too much of a fuss, finally agreeing to our suggestion that we elevate the girl's legs. Two of us propped them up at the ankles on the pew in front. Sister instructed us to carry on with our prayers, reciting our Hail Marys as our classmate lay unparticipatory on the floor. This can't be right, we thought, furtively catching each other's eye. The prayers continued, the same theme as always, pleading forgiveness for our sins.

This was the ground-breaking era of the arrival on the political scene of Britain's first woman prime minister, yet our counsel on leaving school was that the world was an evil and dangerous place and to avoid men and their lecherous ways at all cost. Sexual intercourse outside of marriage was a sin and, just in case there was any uncertainty about what our views on unwanted pregnancy should be, the notice board had a section dedicated to photographs of aborted foetuses.

Many years later, working with a district nurse as part of my nursing training, pregnant young girls came into my care. Seeing their panic and confusion, their lives thrown into turmoil over the very fundamentals of life, I became alert to the danger of ignorance and delegating responsibility. The message from the convent was unrealistic for most people, it didn't allow for failing. There was no advice on what to do if mishaps occurred. The rules were clear: perfection or destitution; in essence, a rejection of human nature and the realities of temptation.

In Mother Bridget's maths class she too wanted perfection. We would sit our test and only those who passed with one hundred per cent would move on to the next level. It was quite a long test as I recall and each time we sat it, a different test each time, many of us would nearly get there, but couldn't quite achieve the full marks she insisted upon. The one or two girls who found maths easy sailed through at the first attempt. The rest of us were left trying. For many it was an unattainable goal. Fortunately, after only a few more attempts, it was the end of term and so the last time with her as our maths teacher. The view that only perfection would do is a tough lesson in life for anyone, let alone someone with a lot more learning to do.

It was a dangerous lesson because it kept us small. At no point did we ever talk about how to discover and nurture our talents, develop our strengths, or make our mark on the world. There was no reflection on how to make the world a better place save through our own personal relationship with the god that the nuns had made their sacrifice for. Essentially the advice was to read the Bible and be a good girl. The tool kit we left school with was to be wary and just say no.

Sister Eugene would begin divinity lessons with the same three questions: 'Where have I come from? Why am I here? Where am I going?' The answers we recited in unison were: 'To know God, to love God, to serve God.' As with so much else that I learned there, I had little understanding of how to do that apart from going to church. There was scant opportunity for discussion. They had no idea how to communicate these ideas to children. Like the Hail Marys we recited without understanding, dogma was learned by rote.

The Catholic girls were under so much pressure that they felt they had to rebel in a way that us 'nons' didn't need to. The ones who lived locally confessed that they went home for their lunch break for a cup of tea and a fag, sometimes not even returning to school in the afternoons. Arriving at school on a Monday morning they would be grilled in class about how many times they had gone to Mass over the weekend. I, like the other non-Catholics, was given up as a lost cause.

I wasn't a troublemaker at school. I didn't rebel. The most mischief I got into was bringing in sweets for the boarders and eating some during maths lessons. There was a run of popularity for aniseed balls, the rock hard ox blood-coloured candy with a shot of aniseed in the middle. On reflection, aniseed balls were not the sweet of choice for eating in class. It was very tricky to answer aloud one of Mother Bridget's maths questions with one of those in your mouth. It would have been much better to go for something like a gummy caramel that you could stick to the roof of your mouth while still managing to speak.

That was fun, but discipline always threatened. Just outside the school one lunchtime, my sister Caroline was caught by Sister Eugene.

'Where are you going?' she asked.

'My mum's given me permission to go into town.'

'Don't you lie to me, child,' Sister replied, slapping her around the face, the slaps in time with the rhythm of the words as she spoke them. 'I'm going to phone your mother and find out,' she said as she reached for the zip of the money belt Caroline wore around her waist.

'It's true, Sister. My mum gave me permission.'

'Give me the money for the phone. Where's your ten pence?' Sister asked, as she tugged again at the zip on the belt.

Caroline wasn't lying, Ma had given her permission. Sister didn't call Ma, it was all fright tactics, but it left Caroline traumatised and angry that she hadn't been believed.

We didn't have an electronic bell system, so classes ended when one of the sisters rang the handbell. One summer's day when we were all outside for break, Sister took hold of the bell and rang it rigorously as she leant out of the window. The wooden handle became separated from the metal bell, which went flying out of the window, barely missing a group of girls on the lawn below. We all stopped and turned to see what had happened. 'That could have killed someone,' a lone voice said. A pupil was sent on an errand to collect the separated piece and no mention of it was made again. Humility was the theme of the Bible reading that day, the perfect opening for an apology that was not forthcoming.

Like our shop, the convent had a cellar. I suppose it would have been a kitchen and pantry once upon a time but now it was our changing rooms. To get down there, you descended a narrow flight of stairs near the back door of the school. A low-ceilinged corridor filtered into two separate rooms with row upon row of looped metal pegs like upside-down double clefs. Wire metal lockers opened beneath a thin wooden bench that ran around the entire room. Here we would perch to change into our indoor shoes, taking off our velour hats and bottle green macs.

Like the cellar in our shop, it felt cool whatever the season. I never felt frightened down in the sweet shop cellar. Even if someone turned the lights off by mistake and you were caught down there in the dark, it didn't scare me. Perhaps it was the familiar smells, the sweet tobacco and confectionery. Perhaps it had always been a happy place. But unlike our cellar, this one made me feel uneasy from fear of the unknown, or rather, the known.

Everyone knew the story of the headless ghost appearing in the huge old-fashioned mirror on the far end wall. It may well have been just a prank made up by boarders at some sugar-fuelled midnight feast but it was established school folklore and, as such, people didn't question, just accepted it.

The light switch was at the top of the stairs. There must have been other light switches in the changing rooms, but in the dark, you would never be able to find them. Much quicker to just make a run for it, back up the stairs to illuminated safety. One day arriving late for school, as I was hanging up my rain-soaked mac, the lights went out. I turned towards the exit in pitch black fear. There was no one down there with me, no one that I had heard. 'Get out, get out!' I felt my body say. I ran towards the exit, feeling for the walls, the cold chalky bumps of the bricks on my hands. I ran up the stairs, three at a time, the heavy pleats of my kilt swinging and swaying, the worn rubber soles of my brown buckled shoes slapping the splintered steps.

'What are you doing?'

My eyes adjusted to recognise the scowling face. 'I'm late! I'm late, Sister!' I replied.

'Children of God don't run!'

'Yes, Sister,' I replied breathlessly. Such a reprimand I could handle. My poor pounding heart told me I had escaped something much worse.

The school itself was a late Victorian Gothic mansion with stained-glass windows of heraldic crests, carved marble chimneypieces, twisted colonnettes and Arabian-style arches topped with a moulded plaster ceiling. An austere house, not one to be fallen in love with, built to reflect the aspiration and achievement of its former incumbents. Its baronial imagery and ornamentation were strangely out of place, self-conscious in their display; the insignia of a family who had long since moved out.

Yet it was once a family home, built for Alfred Pope of the local brewers Eldridge Pope. The brewery itself was less than a mile away and the pungent smell of mash tun would drift across the tennis courts, heady and heavy. The architect was Gerald Crickmay, with whom Thomas Hardy had served his apprenticeship. It could have made a lovely home with its verandah and large bedrooms looking out onto the south-facing garden. A house built for enjoyment with its billiard room (which became the chapel) and gardens set out for playing croquet and taking tea on the lawn.

It was a dominant house, for a dominant family, connected to the community through commerce. At the time it was built Eldridge Pope was the largest employer in the town, its scope reaching out across Brunel's emerging railway network and beyond.

But I knew it only as our school. Running up and down the servants' staircase, chatting on the go to get to lessons after break. The bedrooms in the attic with small windows and lino floors, where servants' beds and wash stands once had stood, now replaced with wooden desks with lift-up lids and bolt-on benches, their inkwells spattered blue. The neat rows looking forward, focused on the smudgy blackboard and teacher's unassuming chair. The wide elegant formal staircase with its huge ornamental balustrade, kept for ceremony (or shortcuts in a hurry) where we would pool around the lower steps for morning prayers in the wood panelled hall. And afterwards, walking back up the grand stairway to step into the warm coloured light, reflected through the stained-glass panels of family pride.

The richly decorated interior was at odds with the message at the core of our education: to shun materialism, and that life, rather than to be enjoyed, was about servitude and acceptance. We received constant reminders of our inadequacies and failings; that we would never be free of the stain of a sinner. Before we could make our mark on the world we had to make amends. Certainly there was little by way of message that life should be joyful, that indulging in passions and interests was a good thing.

We never marvelled at the building or explored its history and links to the town. What of the people who had lived here? A patriotic Wessex family who lost three sons in the First World War. Percy, at the Battle of Loos, his body never found; Charles, drowned when his hospital ship was torpedoed in the Mediterranean; and Alex, who was invalided out and died just after the war.

Where were the telegrams read? In the porch, the library or slumped onto the bottom stair in the hall? Who brought them? The post mistress, who, knowing of her sombre message, moderated her gait and tone of voice, watched by the gaze of the local people to see whose door she was delivering to.

Which are the sacred spaces where so much sadness lingers, that I have walked through oblivious? If I had known, I would have marked them in some way. As with the family, I sense the house grieved, built full of promise, a statement piece, a symbol of successful enterprise, like the haughty butler of a wealthy master, who takes on pompous airs.

A house scarred by sacrifice, left bereft, its family broken. A house designed and built for sanctity and show, stripped of its grand trappings. Gone were the heavy Victorian furniture, brocaded drapes and house plants, rugs and plumped-up cushions. In place of the busy eclectic interior so aspired to by that generation, the floorboards were laid bare, waxed and buffed, administered with care, but only just enough.

The building was powerless, disappointed at its fate, its drop in status from prestigious home to school house. Stoic, respectable, self-sacrificing, it matched our educators' messages for us to a tee.

Because I couldn't start nursing until I was eighteen, I planned to go to Weymouth Tech to do a pre-nursing course and English and French A Levels. The college wasn't a good fit for me, however. Perhaps it was the lack of structure and discipline, but mainly it was my sensitivity to the fact that no one on my course seemed to do any work. Students arrived late for lessons or not at all, and hardly anyone did the homework. The tutors were excellent and I felt embarrassed for them. After the first term I pleaded with Ma to leave. She is always good in a crisis, knowing how to respond. She is not the sort of person to say, 'Just stick at it for another year or so and you'll be fine.' Rather, she listened and found me an alternative place to go. Within a few days I was having a meeting with the headmistress of the local all-girls comprehensive who interviewed me while her dog rather bizarrely leapt in and out of her office window.

I started at the sixth form of Castlefield School a term behind everyone else. I had no choice but to voraciously read the set texts and steadily catch up with the rest of the class. Yet I thrived because this was a place where people were encouraged to have ambition. For the first time I was with girls for whom it was possible to dream big – of becoming doctors, architects, naval officers, and I was inspired. I came out of it at eighteen with my A Levels and a renewed drive, and took up my place to become a nurse.

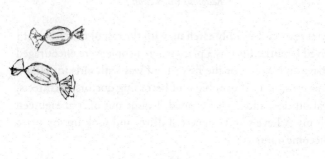

22

House Detective & Decorator

B Y THE TIME I left home at eighteen my family had moved eight times. As you know by now, I am neither a diplomat's daughter nor a brigadier's. My father didn't get posted with his work, neither was he on the run. When I asked him why we moved so many times, he replied, 'Moving creates opportunity.' It was part of the aspirational dream, to own your own house. Moving was a way to upgrade to a better one.

Aside from the Victorian guest house with the tower and ghost, we have had a 1960s box, a bland 1970s estate house and an Edwardian boarding house. We have had a fifteenth-century cottage with wattle and daub ceilings (cow dung and straw) and an eighteenth-century one with violent neighbours who used to come out at night and try to demolish our newly built garage with a sledgehammer. Then later came a Georgian farmhouse complete with ancient Aga and huge cast iron baths that took a week to fill. That was an interesting renovation for Pa. The couple who had owned it had fought, and the husband asked us to look out for the engagement ring that the wife had lost, presumably thrown at him in a row. We never found it.

Buying a house back then was easier than today. Stamp duty was low and you could raise a deposit on a house by selling your car – the first home my parents bought costing less than Pa's brand new 1959 Mini Cooper. That said, Dorset is littered with houses that were once in the running as our family home, the estate agent reassuring disheartened Ma that, 'There's always other properties.' Even so it was difficult to cut the emotional ties where some of the houses had got under her skin.

Some properties were considered for business ventures. The most exciting was Birkin House, a largely unaltered Victorian mansion with nine bedrooms and twenty-eight fireplaces on the London Road not far from Grey's Bridge over the River Frome. The old woman, who still lived there reclusively like Miss Havisham on the upstairs floor, had wardrobes bursting with Victorian clothes. I was desperate to have the house, perhaps more for its contents and magical feel than for the bricks and mortar. I would have liked Pa to have done the place up to live in. But that wasn't feasible; it needed a commercial purpose. Gradually the dreams and schemes faded away as we slowly realised that this was not going to be our next big project.

Going to look at houses as a family we soon learned not to be embarrassed when Pa started jumping up and down on the floorboards. He knew a nightmare could lie beneath even the most well-presented home. He was like Inspector Clouseau with his own investigative routine. You just had to leave him to it. While we were assessing the feel of the place and deciding where we would put the furniture, he was eyeing up how much work there was to be done.

Prodding spongy window frames for signs of dry rot, nosing down cellars for hints of damp, exploring loft spaces for hidden clues, he would emerge with cobwebs in his hair or smears of dust down his back. Nothing got past him, spiders and darkness never put him off. And as for a house with Crittall windows or a flat roof, you would never get him near the place, however desirable the location.

He warned me off a student house once when he saw the tangle of electric wires hanging alarmingly in the shower, and labelled it a death trap. The landlord, delighted to share the provenance of the furniture and fittings, proudly declared that they had come by way of the dump. He had done the electrics himself. I should have seen the signs. The beds were on bricks, and the overgrown garden a burial site for two abandoned Ford Capris. No wonder Pa's practical fault finder was on high alert.

And once the house was bought he would set about carrying out the work. The smell of paint was as familiar to me growing up as the aroma of sweets in our shop; wallpaper paste, new carpets and the heady vapours of Evo-Stik all mingled with oiled Guernsey wool and the great smell of Brut. These are the sensory tramlines that lead me like magic straight back to Pa. He always seemed to have a decorating project on the go. But we loved it; the excitement of coming home from school to see the progress he had made, impatient to see the finished job. Ninety-nine per cent of the work is preparation, he would say, with his broad bushy eyebrows peppered with plaster dust. The finish is only as good as the time you spend rubbing down, filling holes and getting the painting surface as smooth as you can. And it showed. Our window sills were as sleek as silk, coated in gloss paint as thick as double cream.

He knew what it took to transform a dingy inelegant space into a room you wanted to be in. He was a starter-finisher – you start a job, commit to it, push through when the enthusiasm begins to wane, and get it done. Not for him unfinished DIY jobs or half-decorated rooms. He was in his domain, supported by his own skill set, experienced, practised, patient. He was agile as well as skilful, climbing sideways up step ladders without using his hands, as he deftly filled holes in the walls with Polyfilla from an old chipped mug. He wasn't a man to paper over the cracks.

He was a tidy worker. Not for him ladders covered in wallpaper shreds or overalls speckled in paint. He lifted the ladders carefully, not juddering them across the floor. He had respect for his tools, like a sculptor, knowing the beauty his chisels could reveal. He knew the more care he lavished on them the better the result would be. And he looked after them well; none left out in the rain to rust. Patience and consideration seemed to lend a hand of goodwill to the progress of his projects.

If he came to a halt, if a knotty problem stood in his way, if he only had a square peg for a round hole, he would make that square peg round, and perfectly so. He wasn't scuppered by anything. Wattle and daub of a fifteenth-century cottage, Georgian joinery or geriatric plumbing. Nothing fazed him. If you told him something couldn't be done, his mind would immediately go into overdrive to find a way. There is no better example of this than during the power cuts and electricity rationing of the 1970s and the Winter of Discontent. It was hard enough at home, doing homework by candlelight or Ma preparing supper not knowing when the electric oven would cut out, but things were more challenging in the shop. We couldn't just close up when the lights went out, we needed to keep trading. But how do you run a shop in the dark? You improvise, and Pa, being part engineer, draughtsman and inventor, was in his element. He rigged up a set of car headlights attached to a car battery that lit up the whole shop. Pa's contraption wouldn't have looked out of place in the workshop of Caractacus Potts in *Chitty Chitty Bang Bang*, but it certainly did the trick for us. It caused quite a stir in the town. Curious traders and customers came in quizzical and confused.

'How come you've got light, Clive, when the rest of the street's a blackout?'

The answer, as they weren't surprised to discover, was Pa's ingenuity.

'Well, why didn't we think of that!'

The garage was a treasure trove of solutions to any household problem. He wasn't the sort of man to go out and buy nail clippers when he had a garage full of tools that could do the job just as well. I still wince at the memory of him cutting his cuticles with a bare razor blade, and his dismay at the orange stick I proffered. Despite our protestations that he could amputate his nose, he insisted on trimming his nasal hair with an enormous pair of wallpapering scissors. When the gift of a brace of pheasants arrived in need of plucking, he returned from the garage and set to work wearing decorating overalls, dust mask and racing goggles. What else?

I used to enjoy watching him mix cement. The grey limestone dust and sand blended with water from a metal pail that clanged as it made contact with the ground, the rhythmic scraping of the shovel as he got his shoulder behind it. How I admired him, an alchemist of the aggregates. Like a baker mixing dough, he knew the quantities by heart, knew when to add more water. And we joined in as youngsters, though barely able to lift the shovel, the long wooden handle knocking us off balance and clipping us round the head.

Many years later, and totally out of character, he bought a house at auction unseen. He had the idea to do it up and sell it on for a profit. He underestimated how much work was required and it really wore him down. He could renovate anything, and he did, but I think what got to him with that one was that he was kicking himself for not doing his usual due diligence. It was a moment of madness, a temporary lapse perhaps brought on by the thrill of the auction. It is hard to complete a project when you know you shouldn't have taken it on in the first place. We were used to him coming home from auctions with unusual items, but buying a house like this was a first for him. The more likely fare, typically brought home by him on his bicycle, were: a vintage French streetlamp, a brass inlaid tabletop and a pendulum clock in need of repair. He loved having 'a poke about' at auctions. You couldn't take him shopping, but if it involved car parts or historical artefacts in need of some TLC, he would be chomping at the bit.

Aside from auctions, Pa enjoyed some fun with the classifieds in the local paper. Translating the cryptic abbreviations in themselves was part of the fun, created by the fact that the seller paid by the letter. The advertisement needed to give all the necessary information as succinctly as possible: *£500 ono meant £500 or nearest offer, and gwo stood for good working order.* If you were buying a car you would be amazed at the amount listed that apparently had had only *one careful lady owner.* The ads felt secretive, like being in receipt of a coded message from a spy.

I found a second-hand music centre advertised in the local paper and Pa and I drove over to Weymouth to track it down, like a couple of pirates in search of treasure. It was just what I wanted, its tan-tinted Perspex cover setting off the turntable and tape deck, perfect for playing my LPs and compilation tapes recorded off the Top 40. We crowded around it like a couple of old sea dogs trying to deduce whether the treasure was worth our trouble. Yes it was, but at the right price. Fortunately I could rely on Pa to do the deal, he knew the patter, he knew the drill. Shortly we were to be returning home with our goodies, he with the music centre under his arm, me following behind with the two boxy speakers.

Later, I needed a desk for my student house. I found one advertised in Portland. It was a really sturdy affair, solid oak with a heavy metal frame, the sort of desk that looked like it had come from an office clearance, a bank perhaps. Somehow between us we managed to bring it down the stairs and wrestle it into the back of the Renault 16. He helped me cart that desk around to my string of student houses, straining under its weight as he negotiated cramped landings and narrow doorways. Even after I had left home I used to go on my own to buy things through the classified ads. I thought nothing of turning up at some strange bloke's house and brokering a deal in his kitchen. Pa had given me a confidence, a bravado that protected me.

I enjoyed what I bought, but for me the real reward was having Pa at my side as I learned new things, bridging the chasm between childhood and adulthood, dependence and making my way on my own. He made that transition less fearful, more fun. He was in effect the neutraliser of my Catholic teaching that the world was to be feared. Pa bolstered my self-belief and taught me that it was safe to rely on your wits. He was also my safety net, being there when I needed him.

And come to my aid he frequently did, especially where my first car was concerned. He had indulged my desire for my first set of wheels, driving me over to Bournemouth one evening after work to take a look at one that I had clocked in the classifieds. He went against his natural instincts, denied the chance to get it up on ramps in good strong daylight and take a proper look, to cast a mechanic's eye over the whole shebang. But I was so keen to get my hands on my first car that he succumbed to my whim, buying it for me on the spot with the five hundred pounds he had saved.

Its defects had been well hidden in the dusk; the fresh paint job from its close encounter with a post office van that had taken out its entire off-side wing was just for starters. It was a moody motor, leaking oily puddles on his tarmac and a devil to get going on cold damp mornings. Its continental gear stick, a bent-up piece of metal arising out of the dashboard, required a particularly cumbersome movement. But more disruptively, it wasn't reliable, leaving me stranded at various desolate landmarks along the south coast. If I was fairly nearby, I would call Pa, who would drive out to perform emergency roadside repairs and get me back on the road. If I was beyond his reach, I would have to call the AA instead. Either way, the first step to fetch help was to track down a payphone to make the call from – not what you want when it is dark and raining, as it inevitably was.

Yet even when it turned out to be a mechanic's nightmare with parts of the engine seemingly inaccessible, he was philosophical. He knew the deal with cars and it gave us time to chat as I handed him the wrenches or stopped for a break, our oil-clogged fingernails clasped around our mugs of tea.

Occasionally, he wasn't there to help, but he had trained me well. I recall one winter evening, driving home from Brighton to Dorchester, when my front nearside tyre started pulling unnervingly to the left. It was an uncharacteristically stormy night, and the cars whizzing along the coastal motorway seemed to be in a particular hurry to get to where they were going. The wind had been battering my Renault 5, gusting it across lanes when I was overtaking. It had never felt especially stable, more spongy than responsive, swaying around roundabouts like a wobbly blancmange.

I pulled over onto the hard shoulder of the motorway and got out to look at the tyre. What a night to have a puncture; it was wild, the wind whistling past my ears and the lorries thundering by a little too close for comfort. I found the wheel brace as Pa had shown me and heaved the spare tyre out of the boot. As I cranked the brace around the wheel nuts, three came loose fairly easily. But one was firmly stuck. I fought the rising panic, reminding myself of stories I had heard of people lifting incredible weights where their survival had depended on it. I jammed the brace onto the stubborn nut and tried to undo it again, bolstering my determination, but it wouldn't give. So then I stood on the brace, bouncing lightly as I leaned on the front of the car. After a while, to my absolute relief, the nut gave way so that I was able to change the tyre and get myself back on the road. I had watched Pa solve many a knotty problem, taking his time, thinking things through. He never gave up, never said it couldn't be done. Thinking like him got me home that night.

It was only afterwards, seeing the destruction on the news, that I realised the winds were part of what is now called the great storm of 1987, the worst storm in England for nearly three hundred years. If I had known, I wouldn't have travelled that night, but there had been nothing by way of warning of the incoming gale. Later, returning to Brighton, driving along the Old Steine leading past the Royal Pavilion, I saw the damage for myself; trees toppled over as if felled in a massive midnight cull. But the noise was what impressed me the most, the squawking of the birds, united in their unison of protest and outrage at the destruction of their nests and shelter.

My Renault 5 finally gave up the ghost when it was rammed from behind by some joy-riding ten year olds who smashed into it when it was parked outside another student house. It ended up a foot shorter, causing the headlights to bulge out of their sockets like protruding eyes. I had run out of the house at the calamitous sound, and seen the young scraps making a dash down the road. Though I could describe one of the youngsters vividly, I couldn't swear to the police officer that he was the driver. Without that there could be no prosecution and they escaped scot-free. The fact that the family were known to the police didn't serve. Without my certainty no doubt they would continue again. It was probably just as well that I was to be car-less for a while, at least until I could afford something a bit more reliable. Breakdowns and callouts were becoming too regular a part of my driving experience.

But I look back on this time with gratitude; it developed another facet of my relationship with Pa. He became my mechanic, rescuer and teacher all merged into one. At the slightest hint of an SOS call he would be on his way, arriving with a smile and a helpful heart. He didn't make a drama out of it, he just did what needed to be done. He got me home.

23

Family Traits

I AM FASCINATED by the family traits that get passed on down the line; a tendency to favour a certain type of cheese, an enjoyment of classical music, a dry sense of humour. It can be tricky to untangle the cords, to see who is connected to what. But for me, when it comes to Pa, what I think I inherited from him, at least for a while, was his love of speed.

He used to build and race cars, competing at local meets at Brands Hatch in the golden age of British motor racing. His collection of slightly yellowing silver cups is a testament to his skill and passion for the sport. To race what you have built, to be adept at tinkering with an engine to get the most out of it, I can see the satisfaction in that.

John True, his childhood friend, recalls Pa's driving; hurtling down bends too fast, spinning the car around in the road three times then heading off again without stopping or pausing for breath. It was invigorating, at least for Pa if not for his queasy passenger. And when rally driving, acting as navigator, nothing flapped him – I wondered why he was so good at reading maps. On icy days, driving around Kent, John would be instructed to get out and sit on the bonnet to aid the front wheel traction, both of them helpless with laughter. Pa did the same to me one day when the snow was well set in and the steep climb of the road barely passable. I got out and clung to the bonnet as the tyres bit into the crusty compressed snow and we snaked our way up the hill. Wasn't I scared? I don't think so. Whatever he suggested seemed a good idea. He knew what he was doing with cars.

As a young man his first car had been an Austin 7 Special, a great-looking car but, alas, with poor performing brakes. Chasing his dad down Kent's Westerham Hill, coming fast around the bend to a traffic jam, he slammed on the brakes and pounded a wide dent in the chrome bumper of the paternal Morris Minor. He got a telling off for that. He knew how to fix things, though, how to make them work. He had learned that for himself. As a child riding a two-wheeler bike that was too big for him, he had been told by his dad that if he wanted one the right size he had better go off to the tip and find a smaller set of wheels to put on, which he duly did.

In the days when the travelling grocer used to call, Pa and his sister Jean thought it a good ruse to play inside the grocer's van parked outside their house. Pa's mate John joined in the fun. Just to see what it would do, Pa released the handbrake and the van started rolling backwards down the hill. Pa and John jumped out leaving Jean in the van as it crashed its rear end into a neighbour's wall. None of the children were hurt. Despite a thorough telling off it didn't extinguish Pa's fascination with cars.

Something in him rubbed off on me. I am embarrassed to think of the number of near misses I have had down narrow country lanes and the fright I must have given the drivers as they emerged round a bend. Given this pattern of recklessness, it was really only a matter of time before I was to be involved in something more serious.

The freedom of driving a car after passing my test first time was like no other I have ever felt. I was like a greyhound let off a leash. I thought that passing my test meant I knew it all, that I was a safe driver. I only learned later that passing your driving test is just the beginning. The practice continues every time you get behind the wheel.

The first car I drove was Ma's VW Polo. Her eyes and mine looked at it differently; her little runaround was my hot-hatch. One day I took my boyfriend out for a spin.

'If you carry on driving like that, Lucinda, you'll kill us both!' Ed said as I raced along the Dorset lanes. Gravel and mud lay in swathes along the road, washed down the hill by the early morning downpour. I didn't slow down. I had passed my test, I knew what I was doing. The steep banked hedgerows rose high beside us. I motored on, surging along in the valley between, the power of a river with a momentum of its own. Then, as we came over the brow of the narrow hill an Austin Allegro emerged in front of me. The road was too narrow for both of us. I slammed on the brakes and the car started skidding, the mud and gravel neutralising its grip on the tarmac. Dunlop tyres, once used to hugging the road like the posters said, now glided like a sledge on snow.

I opened my mouth to scream, but nothing came out. 'We're going to hit!' Ed yelled as he grabbed the steering wheel, turning it as far and as fast as it could go. Pa used to do that with me when we rode on the bumper cars at the fair, steering me out of trouble.

We lurched to the left, mounting the steep bank lining the lane. We climbed up until we could go no further, the engine starting to complain. If we had carried on we would have ended up in a field. The car then started to roll over on its side, over and over, three times, landing upside-down on its roof in the middle of the road. We were left hanging, the seat belts suspending us like slings.

There was no getting out of the doors, the metal door frames were bent and disfigured where they had been pounded into the ground. The windscreen had smashed into tiny pieces so we crawled out through the window frames. Some of the gritty shards of glass were in my mouth, the rest of it scattered onto the road and over my clothes. I shook it off like sand from the beach.

As we looked at the wreck the same thought went through our minds. 'I'm not sure we should have survived that.'

Ed was a grasshopper of a man; eighteen years old with long lean legs and huge bony feet wearing desert boots that made his feet look even bigger. He was a good guy to hitchhike with as he had the presence to hold his own yet didn't look threatening because of his kind face. I had nearly killed him.

As if by afterthought we checked each other to see if we were hurt. I had escaped with a graze on my right forearm where I had caught the metal frame and still had a few chunks of glass in my mouth. But apart from that I was fine. Ed had not a mark on him.

The driver of the pick-up truck arrived to tow us home. On the way back, he pulled over on the side of the road outside the fish and chip shop to buy his lunch. That was probably the most sobering moment of all; sitting in the cab of the truck with the spatchcocked wreck dangling behind us, waiting for the driver to return with his greasy parcel wrapped in an old edition of the *Dorset Echo*. Were we to make tomorrow's headlines? The wait was delaying the inevitable. What the hell was I going to say to Ma?

The recovery truck sat discreetly out of view as Ma opened the door to see Ed and me standing together. Her initial response to my somewhat understated opener, 'Ma, I've got something to tell you,' was a hug and a non-judgemental welcome. And a tot of brandy.

It wasn't a good move. The policeman who turned up was frustrated that he wasn't able to breathalyse me. I hadn't been drinking, I hadn't that excuse. The driver of the other car was not injured, just shaken. It had been his second accident in a month, neither of them his fault. Ma's car was a write-off and naturally I felt responsible. I don't recall any reprimands or punishments, life carried on as normal. But from that day, the difference in me was huge. I felt that I had been given a second chance and I was determined not to waste it. It created a sense of urgency that perhaps wasn't there before. However young or old I was, life could be snuffed out any second. If I had work to do on this planet, I had better get the heck on with it. But at the same time my second chance encouraged me to play, to treat life like a great big dressing up box; to pick out whatever role or opportunity caught my eye, and try it on for size.

24

Hardy Country

S OME WRITERS ARE associated with specific locations; Beatrix Potter with the Lake District, Laurie Lee with the Cotswolds, and for us in Dorset, Thomas Hardy. But sharing the same locale with a famous author doesn't necessarily give you an affinity with them. It was only because we were good family friends with the then tenants of Max Gate, the Victorian villa he designed and built on the edge of Dorchester, that I became more interested in Hardy. Bill and Vera Jesty were ideal tenants, fully involved in the town and the Hardy Society, welcoming literary guests to Max Gate as Hardy himself had done.

The house is owned by the National Trust, left to the nation by Hardy's sister. When I used to visit it was not then open to the public. Sadly, after inheriting it, she sold off most of its contents so there was very little left that was original. The Jestys did their best with it, making it as much of a home as they could with their own furniture and belongings, and their pet terrier Wessie snoozing by the fire. But you wouldn't call it a warm house, one that wraps its arms around you. It felt like its heart had been cut out, and in a way, it had, twice. It is the place where Hardy fell out of love with his first wife Emma, and where Hardy's heart was literally cut out after he died.

After a courtship that began so passionately in Cornwall, the Hardy marriage faltered as the years progressed. In fact, as the scale of Hardy's literary success grew, their satisfaction with each other declined and Emma removed herself to the attic rooms. Visiting Max Gate one Sunday afternoon, I went up into the attic and had a sense of the loneliness Emma must have felt. Compared to the light and generously proportioned rooms of downstairs, designed with skill by the owner-architect, the attic rooms are as you would expect, an afterthought of basic isolation. Here amongst the eaves, she lived as far from her husband as she physically could, while still living under the same roof. As a further act of defiance she burnt her love letters in the garden.

To me the feel of the house was calculatingly austere, as though I was being weighed and measured by an invisible source. Perhaps it was because the original inhabitants had long critiqued each other, finding fault in everything they said and did. Perhaps such judgement was ingrained in the walls.

The ornamental mirror above the fireplace in the drawing room is one thing that has remained. Standing in front of the fire where Hardy himself would have stood, I have tried to call forth a ghost of the past, the reflection of the 'time-torn man'. But all I could see was my own face, discernible despite the dark spots appearing like mould on the age-tarnished mirror. The mirror had reflected a decaying marriage. Emma with her staunch Victorian views seemed better suited to have been a vicar's wife than that of a writer drawn to the controversial subject matter that she abhorred.

Upstairs in Hardy's study, the feeling of the room was very different; it felt freer and more relaxed. Here he had written *Tess of the D'Urbervilles* and *Jude the Obscure* at his desk beneath the window, with his shoes kicked off to reveal his socks. I would sometimes sleep here in Hardy's study when I came to stay at Max Gate. I would awake in the hope of finding him there, creatively exposed, reading aloud excerpts of his prose, feeling the articulation of the words in his mouth. Later, when I came across the reconstruction of his study at the Dorchester Museum, his desk, his blotter, his pens, it felt surreal to see the room I had slept in, transported there.

And so to his heart. Despite his wish to be buried at his local church at Stinsford, such was the demand after his death for him to be recognised in Poets' Corner in Westminster Abbey that a compromise had to be reached. His ashes are interred at the Abbey, but his heart is buried at Stinsford. When the doctor came to Max Gate to remove his heart, he realised that he had nothing to put it in, so, resourcefully, the parlour maid, Nellie Titterington, provided him with a cake tin. The undertaker collected the tin containing the heart and placed it in the casket, which is buried at Stinsford.

Standing over Hardy's grave at St Michael's Church in Stinsford, the Mellstock of his novels, I've reflected on the memorial he shares with both his wives. Emma, who died first, not only shares her final resting place with her estranged husband, but also with Florence, Hardy's second and much younger wife. I wonder how such an idea would have appealed. To my modern mind it seems an unusual arrangement that Emma would surely neither have envisaged nor desired.

Hardy's name for Dorchester was Casterbridge, the setting for his novel *The Mayor of Casterbridge*. The eighteenth-century house that served as Mayor Henchard's home was just a few steps across the road from our shop, an elegant backdrop for the carol singers who convened there at Christmas time. The Corn Exchange and the clock that I could see from my bedroom window are mentioned in *Far from the Madding Crowd*. It is the location for Bathsheba's swooning into the arms of Farmer Boldwood on hearing news of her husband's drowning. The Corn Exchange in my day was less significant. I remember coming here for a disco, the strobe lighting and frenetic beats feeling incongruous in the high Victorian setting. There was no swooning into anyone's muscular arms as I recall.

To the rear is North Square where the prison used to be. It was also the site of the public hanging of Elizabeth Martha Brown, the last woman hanged in Dorset. Her crime was the murder of her violent husband who used to beat her with a horse whip. Amongst the macabre voyeurs was a young Thomas Hardy, who witnessed the scene and described it in a letter: 'a fine figure she showed against the sky as she hung in the misty rain…and how the tight black silk gown set off her shape as she wheeled half-round and back.'[1] How could such an image not stay with him forever? Did we not meet his memory in his description of Tess who endured the same fate for murdering her cruel and possessive oppressor?

Hardy's skill lies in his characterisation, his realism, his descriptions of the tug-of-war with the elements and the constraints of the age. His influence may feel removed from the comings and goings of modern day Dorset, but if he were to observe its inhabitants, his fascination for their character traits, eccentricities and yearnings would surely be no less acute. I wonder what he would make of our modern ways.

At the top of town, calmly surveying the changing pace of life, there sits a statue of the man himself, who, depending on the jubilance of youth, may or may not be sporting a traffic cone.

---

1 Michael Millgate, *Thomas Hardy: A Biography Revisited* (Oxford, Oxford University Press, 2004)

25

Holidays

THE RETURN FROM our camping holidays to Cornwall was usually signalled by the sight of Pa's Breton cap stretched over a saucepan of steaming water, the obvious solution for it having shrunk in the rain. As time went by we decided to try somewhere a little less hit or miss with the weather. And so we ventured to the South of France.

We came to love our holidays there, although it was a long drive for Pa, and at times, a testing ordeal for Ma, the reluctant navigator. French road signage took some getting used to, often leaving us guessing, as signs to *Autres directions* often seemed to point somewhere in between the choice of two roads. Our guesses sometimes paid off, other times not, and in the days before sat nav, Ma, clueless, would be faced with 'Is it left or right here, Jude?' One time we must have taken a wrong turn just before Paris, missing the *Périphérique* ring road altogether, for as we rose up over the brow of the hill, there in the distance as clear as it is on the postcards was the Eiffel Tower, resulting in our communal shrieks of wonder and surprise. Despite our unintended diversions and attempts at driving through central Paris towing a caravan (not to be recommended), or stopping just short of height restricted bridges, we eventually found our way south.

As we approached Lyon and the air got warmer and the blue of the sky more intense, Pa would pull over and change out of his long trousers and into his shorts. It was a holiday ritual, a sign that we were getting there.

Setting the caravan on our pitch and putting up the awning was always a slightly fraught but fortunately short affair – a final hurdle before we could all relax and start enjoying our holiday. Ma could be relied upon to defuse any frustrations by emerging from the caravan with segments of juicy peaches that we had bought from the vendors at the side of the road. You could taste the sunshine in them as the juice dribbled down your face.

Pa, on the other hand, could be relied upon to rustle up the breakfasts, relishing the enjoyable challenge of cooking in a confined space and the chance to try out the perfect non-stick egg poacher that he had sourced beforehand. He became king of the fry up, master of crispy bacon, crunchy toast and runny fried eggs. His holiday cooking dress code comprised an apron worn over his bare chest, soft denim shorts, sandals with socks, and his Breton cap. How many photographs there are of us tucking into a plateful of his cooked breakfasts, the novelty and sense of occasion showing on our faces.

Days were spent bronzing by the campsite pool and for the evenings we headed out to savour the Riviera restaurants. Strolling around the harbours of Monaco, Cannes and Nice we watched the yachts and tableaux of deeply tanned teenagers darting about precariously on their mopeds. Then we would stop at one of the restaurants and tuck into a plate of *fruits de mer* with a carafe of wine. Life was bliss. 'This is what you work for,' Pa said.

Not all of France's customs were as easy to embrace as others. While we had no problem whatsoever with camping and communal shower blocks it was the Turkish toilets we couldn't understand. It was a mystery to Ma, she would explain, how such a thing could exist in a country renowned for chic fashion. Just how was one expected to do a counter-levered squat on wet slippery porcelain in a pencil skirt? Or, when wearing loose long trousers and having to hoist up the dangling length of fabric at the same time as keeping an eye on where the squirt of wee was heading. Too great an angle and you either got sprayed or could fall down the hole. You wouldn't want that.

This was the type of toilet unsuspecting British holiday-makers used to find on their way to the South of France when they stopped for a break on the *Autoroute*. They are much improved now, some of them even have music playing, but the fact remains, they are a hole in the ground.

Ma had entered the cubicle after a well-intentioned English woman had completed her ablutions. Politely but fatally the woman had held open the door for her, allowing her to slip in before the self-cleansing cycle had had a chance to run. The automatic sanitising mechanism, as those in the know are aware, begins upon closure of the door after the cubicle's use. So, as Ma took the door from the woman and closed the door on herself the lights went out and cleansing began.

Her feet and clothes were soaked by the splurging spray of water and her hair restyled by the rising jet of steam. It was a frightening ordeal, her panic expressed in her cries.

'Press the button, Ma!' Caroline and I shouted.

After sufficient time had elapsed to give both her and the Turkish toilet a thorough clean, the toilet door opened. Stepping forward out of the parting curtain of steam was Ma, leather sandals sodden, skirt clinging soaked to her legs, and hair bouffant; her high colour the result of embarrassment and a steam facial. We couldn't see her eyes through her misted-up sunglasses.

'Oh Ma! Are you all right?'

'Oh Lucinda. It was frightening. I couldn't get out. I couldn't see. Do I look bad?'

'No. No, Ma. Come and sit down.'

As we sat at one of the picnic tables outside and sucked on a soothing boiled sweet we saw what looked like Ma's twin walk by. Another unsuspecting foreigner had endured the same experience. Ma and the woman looked at each other.

'Morning!' Ma said

'Morning,' the woman replied.

English reserve – just carry on as normal.

26

Family Identity

I GREW UP with a strong sense of family identity. I am lucky to have had Ma, a brilliant storyteller, who at the slightest nudge would spill her tales, her memories of her Cornish heritage. Coming back from days out late at night, Pa at the wheel of our Renault 16, the rhythmic flash of street lights falling across the car, illuminating her, Ma would entertain us with her childhood memories. Some of these involved people I had met, some I had never known. But the tales she told brought them all to life for me, to such an extent that if any of them were to walk into the room right now, I would have no hesitation in putting my arms around them and greeting them like I had known them forever. To me, they are not just faceless names on a grid, I feel I know them. They are not just family because they are on my family tree, they are family because they have familiarity. It feels good to know where you come from, to see where you fit in to the larger picture.

Ma's immediate family seem to have come from humble beginnings. The menfolk were rabbit catchers and agricultural workers, the women, cooks and maids. There are carpenters but no landowners. The family on my father's side are lawyers, clerics and diplomats, and even a couple of MBEs, but I knew very little about them when I was growing up because I never learned their stories.

Riding in the car, my sister, who had the gift of falling asleep as soon as she was in motion, dozed gently next to me. She had a survival instinct, conserving and re-charging her batteries when her consciousness was not absolutely necessary. It was the days before we had seat belts in the back, so I would move forward and wedge myself in the gap between the front seats. It was the best place to hear Ma's voice above the engine and road noise.

'Tell me about Grandpa, Ma,' I'd say.

'Oh you've heard it a hundred times before!'

'No, I haven't. Tell me again.'

And so she would begin, retelling her tales, sometimes letting slip a snippet of detail that she had left out before. Snug in the car, protected from eavesdroppers, she shared her secrets. Pa at the wheel, driving us home, listening intently to every word.

Ma's father, Wilson Bunt, my grandfather, was the second youngest of thirteen children, growing up in Bodmin, Cornwall. He used to play the cornet in a trio called The Waldemar Band, three teenage boys looking older than their years dressed in suits and ties. One night they were due to play at a dance at the Public Rooms in Bodmin, but more importantly, the woman Wilson was sweet on, my grandmother, was going to be there. Unfortunately Wilson had got into some sort of scrape and been banned by his parents from going out that night. He persuaded his younger sister, dear Aunt Winnie, to help him climb out of a downstairs window and cover for him. He ran across the fields, cornet in hand, arriving just in time for his solo, 'Moonlight and You'. Grandma heard him play and was smitten. They were married at Lanivet church and held the wedding reception in a field nearby. The photograph shows the bride wearing a simple 1930s dress and veil with flowers in her hair. Stout busty matrons stand alongside wiry men in tired suits while the groom bears the look of romantic responsibility.

The Wilson I knew was a traditional grandfather. Whereas Grandma was more of a fixture in the house, he would come and go, popping in from a trip into town or a pint and game of billiards at the Conservative Club. Dressed in tweed trousers, shirt and thick cable cardigan, he would sit in his fireside chair to doze and be woken with a start by Grandma's call of 'Wils!' if he started snoring a little too loudly.

But one day I did see the fun side of him. Pa was working on the second-hand bike he had bought me to take to my nursing job in Oxford. I had managed to talk Ma out of persuading him to get me a sit up and beg (small wheeled with a basket on the front), for a much racier number with dropped handlebars and ten gears. The joy with Pa was that I didn't need to justify my argument with him when it came to vehicles. He got it. The two options promised a totally different riding experience, and he knew which would deliver better on that front.

Wilson had driven over on an errand in the black Morris 1100, and came into the garage where Pa and I were working on the bike. The BSA bicycle was upended on its saddle and handlebars, where just a moment ago I had been rotating the pedals and oiling the chain.

'You know what BSA stands for, don't you?' Wilson whispered to Pa, but in earshot of me.

He paused a moment to give Pa a chance to reply.

'Bloody sore arse!' Wilson said with a schoolboy smile.

They both chuckled, Pa raising his eyebrows in acknowledgement of a good joke. I had never heard Grandpa say the word blimey, let alone bloody and arse in the same breath. It felt refreshing and grown-up.

Wilson's sister Winnie was the nearest person to an angel to me; she is the kindness person I have ever known. I never heard her speak a cross word about anyone. She was married to Arthur, a gentle and mild-mannered man. They had no children, she being warned off by the doctor from trying for another baby after suffering a miscarriage. I used to think it such a grave injustice that she was prevented from being a mother. One day when she was at the hairdressers one of Winnie's neighbours burst in through the door to make a sudden and unwelcome announcement.

'Quick, Win, Arthur's had a heart attack!'

Popping out from under the dryer hood, Winnie scrambled to her feet and ran off down the road with the neighbour, curlers still in her hair. Arthur survived but never fully recovered.

The following day, the hairdresser called round to Winnie's house, requesting payment for the half-finished wash and set. Each time the story was told, either by Ma in the car or by any of my great-aunts, I felt a sharing of this outrage, the insensitivity. It seemed that all the women of the family still bore the indignation of how callously Winnie had been treated, the day she nearly lost her husband.

Arthur died shortly after. I was about four years old when it was decided that I would be sent to stay with Winnie, on my own, to help mend her broken heart. I recall going to have tea with one of her friends and visiting a market where a monkey sat on my shoulder. I think having me around and the routines I came with kept her sane and busy when grief was at its most raw. I was her distraction and because of that we developed a magical bond. I loved her with a full heart.

She used to work as a dinner lady at the school where Mick Jagger's father was headmaster. She was a brilliant cook, everything homemade and delicious. We all used to love her Cornish pasties, trifle, cakes, Sunday roasts and perfect Yorkshire puddings hot from the Aga. Years later we would all go and visit her in St Austell, staying in the house she shared with her sister Dorothy. When it came for us to leave we would be overwhelmed with sadness. There are cine films of Caroline and me sitting in the back of our red Mini crying our eyes out, so sad to be leaving Winnie whom we adored.

When I was a teenager Winnie gave me her long black velvet shawl and evening bag. She laid them out on her candlewick bedspread for me to see. The shawl has a V-shaped diamanté Art Deco design along its edge, with black and silver tassel trimming. The black velvet evening bag has a diamanté clasp and a velvet handle, just long enough to dangle elegantly from your forearm. She told me of how she had worn them to dances. Inside the bag, she kept her dance card, a list of names of dashing young fellows who had the courage to ask. Over the years I have used them a lot, each time feeling cloaked in a state of excited refinement.

Looking at photographs of my great-aunts and grandmother in pigtails and pinafores, I have stared deeply into the sepia to glean as much of a sense of who they are as I can. Trying to see them as they were then, as little girls, becoming young women, falling in love. The nearest I came to seeing their youthful side was when Winnie and her sister Dorothy came to stay with my grandparents, Marjorie and Wilson. A new dress shop had opened in the town. What I had never fathomed, although they always looked smart with make-up, neat hair and shoes, was their love of fashion. Coming home with their choices, new dresses and jewellery and trying it all on was just like how Caroline and I behave when we have been shopping; showing each other what we have bought, having our own mini fashion show. I had always perceived them as old, but in that moment I saw their youthfulness, their sense of fun, a glimpse back to when they would dress up to go out on a date or a dance.

When Dorothy died, she left her house to her son with a life interest to Winnie, who had sold up her own house and moved in with Dorothy when her husband Arthur had died. Although the provision in the will was for Winnie to stay there until she died, Dorothy's son had other ideas. 'You don't want to stay here on your own, Win, the place is too big for you,' he said to her each time he came round, during his more and more frequent visits. We went up to stay with her, to help her stand firm. Winnie would fight back the tears as she told Ma and Pa the latest, of the pain of feeling unwelcome. I felt dedicated to her cause and pleased to be part of the reinforcements that had arrived. She later moved out to a one-bedroom flat, unable to take the emotional pressure any more. He got the house, and died not long after of a heart attack.

Wilson and Winnie's mother, Grannie Bunt, Ma's grandmother, had brought thirteen children into the world. She had spent most of her adult life either pregnant or nursing a child. In her declining years, fading and worn out, she took to rocking with her arms wrapped around herself, calling out the name Sidney, the one child who hadn't survived. Seeing her distress, one of the family borrowed a doll from a little girl who lived along the road, wrapped it up in a shawl and gave it to Grannie Bunt to hold. Perhaps as her own death loomed, she felt closer to the child who had died before her.

Ma would tell stories of the thirteen children, the beautiful daughter who became pregnant by the so-called 'young gentleman' of the big house, where she was a housemaid. All was hushed up, my aunt sent away to have the child somewhere quiet. Another of the sisters, Hilda, who was also in service, fell in love with one of the servants and eloped, emigrating to Canada where her family still live. I can imagine the sense of possibility, of young love and the thrill of a new life overseas set against the sadness of saying goodbye to the family that you fear you may never see again. Many years later when Hilda was in her eighties she did try to return home. All packed up and ready for the journey she had a heart attack in the hall, slumped over her suitcases and died.

Whereas Ma's father Wilson came from a large family of thirteen children, her mother Marjorie was one of just two, her older brother Fred and herself. Marjorie's father, Thomas, had died when she was only eighteen months old and her mother Lizzie, though remarrying many years later, never had any more children. Thomas was a roofer. A slight slip on a Cornish slate roof cost him his life at the age of thirty-four and left Lizzie with two young children to bring up and a farm to run.

Marjorie's brother Fred drowned when he was twenty-six. He was engaged to be married to a young local woman. The family story is of a good-spirited young man, a keen learner with a sharp wit and aspirations for a better life. The only photograph I have ever seen of Fred is of him as a three year old, already fatherless, standing in a sailor suit, his boyish face set off by an abundance of thick dark curls.

He had gone to Spit beach, near Par in Cornwall, on his motorbike, with his fiancée and his friend Henry. It was 4 August 1930, Bank Holiday Monday, around lunchtime. Marjorie and Wilson, who were courting then, travelled with them on another bike. Fred motored on down to the beach and dived into the sea ahead of Henry. His fiancée remained on the shore. Marjorie and Wilson stopped to sit on a bench overlooking the sea. Perhaps they wanted time on their own, to make plans for an evening dance, or longer term, to talk of marriage. They could see Fred swimming and then he started waving, larking about as usual, enjoying the late summer sea. They waved back.

And then pausing mid-conversation Marjorie said, 'Where's Fred gone?'

Stricken with the sense that something was not right, Marjorie looked to Fred's fiancée on the beach, who looked back at her with concern on her face.

'He was right there,' their expressions said, expectant in hope of seeing him pop up from the waves, messing about, just one of his pranks. But nobody came up out of the water. He had been drowning, not waving.

The newspaper cutting I have found describes how a Mr Alfred Blight, of St Austell, swam out to Fred when he realised he was in difficulty. But when he reached the spot, some two hundred yards from the shore, there was no sign of him. He searched for a long time but he couldn't find him.

Henry too had got into difficulty, but managed to get ashore. He told the reporter that Fred was the better swimmer but had been further out. The sea was heavy running and the tide was ebbing.

Marjorie left the beach heartbroken. Leaving without someone, not knowing where they are. How do you leave? What time do you leave? How long do you leave it? Knowing that you are going to be the bearer of the worst possible news anyone could ever hear.

Fred's body was found two days later washed up onto Par beach, wedged between rocks. He had had rheumatic fever as a child, leaving his lungs weakened. Perhaps he had got caught in rip tides and hadn't had the strength to swim. His mother Lizzie went to identify the body.

Marjorie had not come from a large family. She had lost her father without chance of knowing him. And now it was just the mother and daughter. She was Fred's younger sister, never ever envisaging that she would stop being the youngest and become the only child. But with him gone, that is what she became, bumped up in her seniority, the one remaining.

I have Fred's walking cane. It is fine and slight and fairly short like a child's. I don't know what wood it is made from but it is very strong and light. It has a fine silver tip over the end of the handle. I like to hold it, not only because it is a beautiful thing and feels nice in my hand, but because it makes me think of the hands that have held it, Fred's, Lizzie's, Ma's and others I don't know. I can imagine it being used out on the cliff paths to hold back brambles or flick away an adder. When Ma used to stay at Lizzie's farm, Oke

174

Woon near Bodmin, as a little girl, Lizzie would never let her go walking without a stick.

'Where's your stick?' she would say as they set off in their boots onto Goss Moor. One day Ma reached down to pick some wild strawberries and her grandmother shrieked, pushing away her hand.

'Not there! There's an adder's nest there!'

She seemed to know everything about the country.

Lizzie never got over what happened to Fred. One night Marjorie woke up to find the front door wide open. Going out into the lane in her dressing gown, she heard her mother's footsteps on the path. She had been down to the cemetery.

'I was just checking it's true, Marjorie, that he's really gone. I saw him in my dream, I thought he was alive.'

After that she repeated the trip to his grave many times, often in the middle of the night. She used to take Fred's silver-tipped walking cane with her, the one I have next to me as I write. The cane is worn at just the place where you put your thumb. It feels smooth and comforting. I don't know whether it's worn smooth by Lizzie's hand after Fred had died, or by Fred when he used to walk the cliff paths, holding back the gorse. Either way I am very pleased to have it.

I also have two old encyclopaedia volumes that belonged to Fred. I don't know where he would have got them. Perhaps they were a gift. The spines are cracked and falling to pieces now but the pages and pictures inside are in good condition. Did he sit and ponder them on Sunday afternoons? The legacy of a silver-tipped walking cane and a set of books conjures up for me a picture of a man who enjoyed life and wanted to get on.

Lizzie lived to be seventy-eight. Marjorie found her dead in her chair by the fire; she hadn't been dead long, her body still warm. After her funeral, Lizzie's farm was auctioned off, the contents of the farmhouse and outbuildings itemised and laid out on the stone floor of the yard. Her crockery, her cups and plates, her cattle and her plough, her old bedstead and mattress, reduced to lots in an auctioneer's catalogue. The old faithful plough horses, Violet and Flower, were led away by their new owners. Amongst her possessions, found stuffed at the back of a drawer, was a carefully folded handkerchief holding a handful of Fred's jet black curls.

I have Lizzie's old copper harvest kettle, saved from the auction. It used to sit on the range in the farm kitchen in constant use. At harvest time she used to take it brimmingly boiling straight off the range and out to the fields for the farmworkers to have their tea. When Ma used to stay with her as a little girl, she would go with her in the jingle, the two-wheeled horse-drawn pony trap.

'Mind you don't touch the kettle, it's very hot,' Lizzie would say, as she flicked the whip and drove the pony and trap forward. I like the idea that the kettle would have been greeted with joy by the workers, marking time for a break from toil to sit and rest, perhaps to chat and discuss the weather or the day's progress, sipping tea and eating a homemade scone or slab of saffron cake.

It is not just a kettle, it is much more than that. It links my great-grandmother to her farm, to the simple daily rituals of life – to me. It is not a luxurious thing and although it is made of copper and looks rather special it was essentially functional and served a purpose over many, many years. I like the patina, I like the smoothness of the handle, I like the signs of wear and tear. I like the dents where it has been dropped and the scorch marks on the base where it has been put too close to the fire. I like the hollow drum sound the lid makes when you put it on, so different from the sound of a modern plastic kettle.

I have a photo of Lizzie sitting on a tree trunk at the farm looking stoic and capable. Her hands are those of a woman who has laboured all her life, hands that are contorted with age yet useful still. Despite her age she still looks strong, a woman in her seventies who wouldn't have had too much difficulty in bringing in the cows for milking single-handed or saddling the old mare for ploughing. As I look at the photo of her and remember the stories, I am very aware that she is of a different era, a different century. Her life looks so much more vulnerable, the basic challenge of daily survival constantly on her mind. And yet of course I don't have the whole picture. I see mostly hardships – the things she lacked like central heating and boiling hot showers, tumble dryers and a car on the drive. I wish I could feel what she had, to know the extent of her joy, her family, her level of contentment. Am I more like her than I know? That's the stuff that both fascinates and eludes.

I have been to Fred's and Lizzie's graves. My son Sam and I looked for them when we were in Lanivet on a family holiday to Cornwall when he was about seven or eight. Looking across at the church where Marjorie and Wilson were married, we stumbled around respectfully over the uneven ground, the grass so long you couldn't see your feet. We had to feel our way, sliding our shoes over the soft round mounds of earth or hard angular pieces of fallen headstone. And then he found it, his young eyes alert to the lettering.

'Here she is, Mummy, Elizabeth Arthur.'

He picked a flower from the hedgerow and placed it on her headstone. And then we found Fred, buried near her. I realised then that on that overgrown spot where Fred's remains lie, now omitted from the graveyard maintenance rota, forgotten by so many, my grandmother and my great-grandmother would have stood. And who else, I wonder?

How can you have sadness for people you have never met? And yet I think that is what family is, that bond of closeness exists whether I have known them or not; they are my family. I think there is always the temptation to grab at the tiniest snippets of information about people and then embellish their stories. You see the tip of the iceberg and make up the rest. Maybe I am on the right track and maybe I am not, but to me it doesn't matter, because I have no truth, I have no guide here apart from the stories I have learned and the depth of love I feel. What I do know is that keeping someone alive in your heart is the greatest comfort of all.

27

Pa's family

WHEREAS MA WAS the storyteller, Pa was more reticent. He very rarely spoke about his family tree. I have learned a little about it, but mainly through my own research or through questioning my aunts. Some families just don't talk about their family heritage, I suppose. I know now that Pa's maternal grandfather was Captain Arthur Bayford Heron, a member of the Royal Army Medical Corps in Palestine who was awarded an MBE for his work there. Apparently, on being posted to Palestine he was told that he could take with him just his wife and two of their four children. His wife refused to go with any of the children, so Arthur Bayford went on his own, and from then on the family lived separate lives. I have since seen photographs of him in his army uniform during the First World War, wearing knee-length leather boots with spurs, on a sturdy-looking horse. Another shows him as an older man, in a more casual pose, sitting on a wall in white trousers and brogues and what could pass for a smoking jacket, as he leans back slightly, taking a draw on his pipe. Pa's grandfather on his father's side was a last-maker in the boot-making business, and by all accounts a lovely man, although he never knew him. Pa never spoke a word about any of them.

I encouraged him to write down memories of his own childhood after my son Sam was born, which he started to do, the pages of which I have included at the end of this book. The photographs of Pa as a youngster give little away, the baby in a baggy knitted romper suit, the young teenage boy at the seaside in what looks like his school uniform, and one of him aged about four, in the park with a leather football that looks heavy enough to blunt his toes. I wish I had asked him more.

Stories make our connection deeper. Without them, names on a family tree are just that. It is the memories passed down that keep people alive.

28

Grandma's home

MA AND PA would have known Dorchester, at least in part before they took on the shop, as Ma's parents lived there. It is also the town where they got married. Marjorie and Wilson's three-bedroomed semi on Prince of Wales Road, while modest, was fascinating to me because it so markedly belonged to a much older generation. In the hall was a telephone bench complete with padded seat and pull-out panel with waxy pen for writing down messages. It made answering the phone an occasion, like having your very own telephone booth in your home. It was so much nicer than the public phone boxes that smelt of fag ends or urine, with their slots for pushing in your two pence piece under panic of the pips. And the heavy metal doors heaved open with your body as a brace, which then pinched closed slowly like a vice. The one outside Weymouth station is where Caroline lost the top of her finger. After returning from a day out in London, Ma stepped inside for a second to call a taxi and the little tinker, eager to stay with mummy, curled her finger around the edge of the colourful cubicle as the closing door sheered its end off like a knife. Ma picked up the severed piece and wrapped it in a hanky for the ride to hospital; Caroline's screams must have been heard all over town.

Grandma's front and back room changed their purpose depending on the season. In winter the front room was used more, in summer the back, with its outlook over the garden. It was a very practical house, everything of use and having its place; the corner where her Singer sewing machine sat and opposite the cage for Peter the budgie; the pull-out leaf table with embroidered tablecloth and mats with horse-drawn carriage scenes, silver cruet, and jar of Branston pickle which came out for Sunday tea. And outside, a verandah with a sloping glass roof where the washing line hung. The garden beyond was laid out to grass with beds of hollyhocks and wigwams of sweet peas, in purples and pinks. Some of the flowers seemed to have a tale of their own to tell; love-in-a-mist, forget-me-not and lily of the valley. A water butt collected rain from the garage roof to be poured into the little watering can and then onto the flowers. But never in full sun, always after sundown or it would deny the flowers their drink, the water being evaporated by the heat.

There was a gramophone in the back room; not like Ma and Pa's boxy blue number – this one was concealed in an elegant wooden sideboard. Tom Jones was Grandma's favourite, especially 'Green, Green Grass of Home'. When the song 'Tie a Yellow Ribbon Round the Old Oak Tree' was popular, Caroline tied a remnant of ribbon around the gnarled old apple tree. It was as if she had brought a touch of magic to the garden, which delighted Grandma and her visitors who joined in together, singing the song.

She had a small vegetable patch, an area dedicated to the growing of onions and cabbages, but she hated the cursed slugs and snails that helped themselves too greedily to her produce. Snails got picked up by their shells and thrown against the garden wall, and when the ants became a problem, kettles of boiling water flushed them away. The blackbirds, on the other hand, were more welcome guests, especially the one she named Blackie who she would chat to and leave out bacon scraps for as a treat.

While the downstairs rooms felt communal, upstairs felt like a different house. The bathroom, a functional room not meant for lingering, was chilly in winter even with the pull-cord electric wall-heater turned on. A peek inside the medicine cabinet found it filled with accoutrements appropriate to her age: coal tar soap, denture pots, Steradent tablets, bunion pads and rusting tins of talc. And on the window sill, a bright blue bottle of Milk of Magnesia. These were the same things to be found in my other grandparents' house, and Winnie's too, although at hers the fascination was the soft bubbling water that foamed out of the Cornish tap, a novelty after the chalky hardness of Dorset.

But what was most striking was a huge black and white panel above the bath of a flock of flying cranes or swans, hovering over a marshland of bulrushes and long wavy grass. There was nothing in the rest of the house that reflected this taste, this level of ornamentation, and it was made all the stranger because the only time I ever saw it was when I was locked in the bathroom on my own. We never had a bath here, even when occasionally we stayed the night.

There was another WC just outside the back door with red ochre brick walls, a wooden seat and Izal toilet paper dispensed in most inconveniently small folded squares. Although the paper was silky smooth, like tracing paper, once you scrunched it up in your hand it became like a Brillo pad. Who would design such a torturous thing? I never wondered why the toilet was outside, it was just how it was at Grandma's.

But the most bizarre thing was her Christmas tree. Barely two feet tall, artificial with prickly needles, it was in a poor state of repair when we first started to decorate it. Several of its branches had fallen off and needed to be stuck back into the trunk with tape. But as each year went by, it became even worse, to the point that there was more sticky tape holding it together than tree. Caroline and I would laugh ourselves silly as we tried to cover it with the decorations of half bare tinsel and bells made out of whisky bottle lids as more and more of the branches fell off. The angel on the top was the best bit, made by Grandma herself, a tiny doll dressed in hand-sewn clothes with a pair of satin wings. And the decorated egg shells, painted with pink and lemon food colouring, suspended on bits of ribbon.

She saved everything. Our birthday presents were wrapped in recycled wrapping paper, sealed with red butcher's tape left over from Grandpa's work. It was just what she did; she would unwrap our birthday gifts to her, usually tins of talc and cakes of soap, carefully to avoid tearing the paper, so that she could save it to use another day. She not only kept the wrapping paper; when she died we discovered that she had stockpiled most of the brand new toiletries too. I suppose when you grow up in a world that is make do and mend, when you are chastised as a child for being wasteful, you never grow out of it.

Everything in the house had a purpose, nothing was frivolous or just for fancy, except for her collection of ornamental dolls that never came out to play. We only saw them when they emerged for dusting, how we longed to play with them, especially the little native American dolls in their beaded tasselled tunics. They looked so bored staring out of the glass china cupboard, lined up with each other in rows.

The beds were very different from ours with duvets back home. Here they were made up with candlewick bedspreads with loops that caught round your toes, silky eiderdowns that you could pull up over your ears and soft pillows that puffed up round your head. And in winter, they were heated by an electric blanket. Oh the joy to snuggle into a pre-warmed bed in a room cold enough to see your breath.

And in the morning she woke us up with a cup of tea, although always with our special request of 'no bits'. We had learned about that the hard way, gulping down a mouthful of tea leaves lurking in the dregs.

Upstairs was calm, no radio, TV or music save the industrial tick of a pair of metal alarm clocks sitting by her and Grandpa's beds; their magnified numerals, fluorescent hands and the deafening din they made when they went off, suggestive of an over-zealous effort to make their presence known.

We used to come over for tea, sitting up straight at table, not speaking with our mouths full, a laundered napkin from a silver ring on our laps. We never had meals on trays, though often one of her freshly baked currant buns could be enjoyed on a plate on the sofa.

Winnie might come to stay for a week in the summer with her sister Dorothy. Taking a break from helping with the chores, they would sit in stripy deckchairs sipping cups of tea under the apple tree. As I watched them laughing and chatting, the pains and gripes of arthritic joints a distant memory, I saw that they were more than just three old ladies; they were sisters and dear, dear friends. If I could go back and meet them again, this is the moment I would choose, carefree like in the song they used to sing, locking arms and smiling, 'Here we are again, happy as can be, all good pals and jolly good company.'

And so from this house Ma left for her wedding at St George's Church. A wedding in February, with snow on the ground so thick that some of the guests were unable to attend, sending telegrams of good wishes instead. And the reception at the Antelope Hotel in South Street, just along from our shop. It had been a seventeenth-century coaching inn and the wagon-wide walkway linking up to Trinity Street behind was living day evidence of that. The photograph of Ma and Pa cutting the three-tiered wedding cake shows two youthful faces, the bright light of the flash capturing Ma's surprise, as if she has turned her head suddenly; her eyes sparkling as brightly as the white of her shoulder-length veil. And Pa's face, bare of the beard he is yet to grow, all smiles. The jerky cine film shows Pa driving them away in the Mini after the reception, a just married sign hanging off the bumper, though it doesn't reveal the gorgonzola and kippers secreted onto the manifold by the mischievous best man.

It was perhaps not the most obvious choice for a wedding reception given its bloody history. The Oak Room at the Antelope Hotel was where the infamous 'hanging judge', Judge Jeffreys, condemned many supporters of the failed Monmouth Rebellion to death in 1685, to be hanged, drawn and quartered, their rotting carcasses displayed in the street. The dubious historical association aside, their Dorchester wedding was a joyful milestone, staking their connection to the town.

My own wedding was what I had wanted it to be. Christchurch Priory, near Bournemouth, is the longest parish church in the country and walking down its aisle with Pa gave me chance to savour the moment. Pa welcomed the task I had asked of him, to source the wedding car, ideally an open top vintage Rolls-Royce. He didn't disappoint. He pulled up behind one at the traffic lights one day, and leapt out to tap on the driver's window.

'Do you do weddings?' he asked hastily, the driver wearing a peaked cap and the car adorned with ribbons.

'You getting married?'

'No, not me, my daughter.'

At which point the traffic lights changed and Pa just had time to be handed a business card through the window before the Rolls-Royce drove forward and out of sight. Pa dashed back to his car, behind which a stream of stationary vehicles were forming and starting to toot their horns. He was delighted with his find. It was perfect, a 1930s Phantom II Rolls-Royce in gleaming cream and chrome. We would enjoy riding to the church in that.

I had wondered what Pa would say to me on our journey together to the church; some words of advice, something he had prepared perhaps. He too was clearly looking forward to having a good chat – but not with me. He spent the entire time enquiring of the driver whose car it was, how many miles per gallon it did and where he went for spares. On reflection, why would I expect anything different? Cars were his passion. I was getting married, not leaving the country. He could speak to me anytime.

He knew more about love than I had credited. When I split up with my long-standing boyfriend, I told Ma and Pa together. Ma was doing the talking, reassuring me that time would heal, that life would go on. But I wasn't ready to move on. Pa just listened. And then, when the talking was over, he squeezed my hand and said, 'I know, it hurts.' It warmed me to the core. He was the only man in our all-girl household, even the guinea pigs and family cat were female (despite their names of Starsky and Hutch, and Snoopy). He left the emotional stuff to Ma, often getting up to leave the room, to 'leave us girls to it'. He left it to Ma because he assumed, naturally, that she would be better at it than him. But he too had wisdom to share. He knew what love was.

Ma's family all loved Pa, they couldn't help themselves. Grandma and Grandpa, Winnie and her sister Dorothy, they all adored him. Winnie's husband Arthur had been a mechanical engineer like Pa. One day he announced to Winnie that a bright new apprentice had started at his work, a very likeable fellow. When Ma brought her new beau round for tea to meet Winnie and Arthur, all became clear. Pa was that man. He was warming to Ma's family before he had even been formally introduced.

Grandma cherished him. She would be caught looking up at Pa with loving eyes.

'What is it, Mum?' Ma would ask.

'He is a lovely man,' she would say, the words smiling out

of her, causing little apples of joy to form on her cheeks. She would spoil him, making him pasties and warm scones, and offering him seconds before he had finished the first lot. He was her family, embodying the men in her life she had lost, her father and her brother. He looked out for her, fixing things, sorting and smoothing her life.

And so it was fitting that he should be the one to find her when she passed away. She had moved in to live with us for the last years of her life. One late December day, taking her a morning cup of tea, he found her half out of bed, stretched across the mattress in her nightie, as though she were just getting out to say her prayers, her face still warm. It was as if she had planned it; she trusted him with the task of gently breaking the news to Ma.

29

Closing Down

ONE DAY WHEN Grandpa Wilson happened to be in the shop when it was heaving with summer exchange students, holidaymakers and regulars, he said to Ma, 'Now is the time to sell. You should sell while it is at its peak.'

They were wise words indeed, but if you sell what else do you do? Perhaps they would have been better to have sold up then, given what happened later, but it is a tough decision to decide at which point you let go of the enterprise you have created, that supports you, and risk it all on a venture new.

She discussed it with Pa but they decided against it. 'No,' they thought, 'everything is going well for us. We have just built a house, we have nice holidays, we have got a good life. If we sell up, what do we do instead? We're only fifty, not ready to retire.'

About six months later something happened. The lease on our shop was always cause for concern, as it came up for renewal every seven years. We had no control over it and Pa held his breath at the time of any rent renewal, awaiting the new terms. The freehold was still in the Walker family, who had run the sweet shop before us, when it was called Florestine's. The Walkers knew the turnover capability of the shop and had the business sense to keep any rent increases at a manageable level. When Mrs Walker died her son Ron, who had run the fruit and veg shop, inherited the freehold. Not long after his inheritance he came out to our house to discuss the lease. Ma was in the middle of cooking dinner, a couple of sirloin steaks that she had been savouring. Ma offered him her piece of steak, which he lapped up.

'You're safe with me, Clive. Nothing is going to change. I'll look after you,' he said as he shook hands on the good intention.

The next day Pa received a letter from an insurance company saying that they had bought the freehold and that the lease would increase from £9000 to £23,000 per annum. Ma and Pa could have fought it in the High Court but they weren't up for the fight. They decided that they would have to close down and sell off the stock. They assumed no one would want to buy the shop as a going concern with such a high annual rent. Anyone taking that on would have to have an astronomical turnover.

'We've had fifteen good years, Jude,' Pa said. 'It is time to go.'

'Yes, Clive, but I can't believe I gave him my steak!'

Winding down a business is a slow death. Slowing it all down to a halt until the natural heartbeat and rhythm have stopped is like putting an animal to sleep when it still has life left in it. But it would not go under easily. Its desire to carry on was strong. Going through the motions, the normal everyday routine of opening up, serving customers, speaking with people as usual. But the usual patter was punctuated with extra stuff, the answers to questions, the things people said. Goodbyes are hard.

'Sorry you're going.'

'It won't be the same without you.'

'All the best, Clive, Judith, see you around.'

Like a terminal patient not knowing whether today would be its last, we would carry on until the stock ran out, when there was nothing left to sell. In many ways it was a letting go of normal everyday practice; we had never let the shelves look so bare, let the stock run so low. This felt like madness. It didn't make sense, the demand was still there. 'What were we doing? What have we done? Can't we just carry on, change course?' But we were on a course with a mind of its own, like sailing with a captain determined to scupper the ship.

The winding down, the selling up, which was it, up or down? It felt like a rollercoaster. We were torn between not wanting it to end and wishing to get it over with fast. We were burning bridges and there was no way back.

There was none of the excitement of those first few days, the opening of the shop, the new phase of our lives. We were breaking up. We were all behind the plan, none of us out to jeopardise its completion, but still, like a family pet that no one really wants to put down, someone has to do it, to make the decision for the rest. And the rest will go along with it, but not in their hearts.

It was a decision made with a forced hand. We wouldn't have run the shop forever, we wouldn't have wanted to, but to go when we weren't ready seemed unfair.

I had felt insulated from what was going on in the rest of the country and the world to a large extent. There were things on the news of course: the city riots in Brixton and Toxteth, IRA bombings, unrest in the Middle East. I had known power cuts, but they didn't cut into my livelihood. Now we had got caught up in a bigger national story, the disappearance of the little shop. Privately owned specialist shops, characterful and individual. When we first came to Dorchester it had a village feel. If you wanted a carpet, you went to see Michael Dench because he was the carpet man in the town. If you wanted leather goods, you went to Templeman's or, for saddlery, to Miles and Son. Furniture was at Wood's up the road, and if you wanted a suit you would go to Mabb's, preferably when their sale was on. Shops were different, as unique as the personalities that worked in them. The high street was specialist, interesting, eccentric. Now I fear it's just bland.

Coming back, would you be able to see evidence of our shop having been here? Like ancient graffiti on the walls, had we left our mark? 'Life goes on,' Grandma used to say. Sometimes it goes on without you. We were the last custodians, at the tail end of the good times. Our time ran out. Progress was juggernauting its way. Bigger is better, more corporate control, more powerful yet more removed. Selling people what they don't really want. Our customers were perfectly happy with the old model. They didn't want reinventing.

But it was our time to go. And perhaps that is the lesson. Why do we expect everything we start to have a completion date under our control? Events take over, unexpected twists in the road, things loom up that we had not spotted. The art is to take it on the rise, to know when you are beat. There is no shame in that, to go out with a bang. I'm not sure we did that.

We made our final farewells with people we weren't in the habit of making arrangements to see from one week to the next, because they used to come into the shop so regularly. By closing down we were shutting off the chance of us meeting again; from now on our paths were unlikely to cross.

Yet our lives had become entwined with theirs, we were meshed together, weft and weave. Our days would feel strange without them and theirs too would be jarred, the gaping hole on the high street where once our shop had stood. But then, as a patch of ground in a garden, nature takes over and covers the space unseen. It just needs a tug at remembrance, a reminder of what has been. Perhaps one day someone will say, 'There used to be a sweet shop there. I wonder what became of them.'

We sold off everything, even the dustpan and brush. Ma used to stay late into the evening bundling together fifty envelopes with elastic bands so that they could be put out for sale in the morning. Everything was discounted, everything had to go. There was a queue outside the shop when we opened. Queues at the till during the day. People bought anything, some of them just wanting souvenirs. It all went. The out of season Christmas decorations, display units, the cuckoo clock. The empty sweet jars.

And then it came. Pa said, 'Right, that's it, we are done here. We've sold all that we can sell.'

After our shop closed down Mrs Eyres retired and Ma helped Julie and Irene find other jobs. Julie went to Marks & Spencer while Irene joined WH Smith. Life at the bigger stores was a very different experience, with far greater formality, targets and rules, where everything was ordered by head office and no one had a clue what stock was on its way.

'It wasn't the same,' Julie said, 'we wished we were back at Osmond's.'

In fact, that's what each one of them told me when I caught up with them, when I was researching this book. I realised what a perfect fit they had been; their sense of fun and mischief, their loyalty and kindness. We had bonded well as a group.

'It didn't feel like you were going to work, it was fun. We weren't treated like employees, we felt like family,' Julie said. 'Your mum and dad never asked anyone to do anything that they weren't prepared to do themselves. Everyone mucked in, whether it was sweeping up or hoovering the floor, cleaning the window displays or putting out the rubbish. Everyone joined in.'

I knew very little about Mrs Eyres when I worked with her, probably because she was much older than me. Arriving at her house I had a sense of déjà vu.

'Have I been here before?' I asked.

'Yes, I used to take you and your sister out to the swings and bring you back here for your mum or dad to collect after they closed up the shop.'

It's funny what you don't remember, the kindnesses you are shown as a child. It must have been a great help in those school holidays when Ma and Pa were both working.

As I looked into her alert watery eyes, a woman of ninety-four years, I realised she had genuine affection for Ma and Pa.

'I loved working in your shop,' she said.

Attending her funeral just a few months later, I heard in the eulogy that she married her first husband at the start of the Second World War, falling pregnant just before he went off to fight. He was killed in action. Her daughter, who delivered the eulogy, never met her father. Mrs Eyres later married a boy she had been at school with in Sherborne, who had always had a soft spot for her. During the war she had worked as a bus conductor in London, which must have been quite a culture shock from rural Somerset where she had lived. As the words of the eulogy sank in, the meaning made sense. The calm capable air that she had exuded reflected a woman who had seen more of life than I had imagined; she was unfazed and valued the present moment.

I was pleased that I had gone to meet her not long before she died. I am glad I found out that she was happy working for us. It made me think that if Ma and Pa hadn't taken that risk, hadn't embraced the opportunity with the shop, they would never have met the people who worked for us and had such an impact on their lives, as they did on ours.

'Working in Osmond's were some of the happiest days of my life.'

All three of them said that to me, Julie, Irene and Mrs Eyres. They all remembered the fun and sense of family. Ma says the same.

'They were good days, hard work, yes, but we did have a lot of laughs.'

30

Last Word

P A DIED A year to the day of being diagnosed with malignant melanoma, ten years after we sold the shop. He was sixty years old and, up until becoming ill, was fitter than most twenty year olds. Ma and I, both former nurses, looked on helplessly aware from the start of the desperately poor prognosis. From the first day of investigation to the last he received only bad news. As each scan returned its findings, further hopelessness was conveyed. He passed away on 18 December 1997, the day after his mother.

When the first rumblings of disquiet about his health came, Ma would petition my opinion on his diagnosis. Behind closed doors she would whisper, 'It doesn't sound good, does it? What do you think?' He had found a lump in his armpit and Ma, with all the training of a professional nurse, had calmly encouraged him to see the doctor and so set in motion the referrals to specialists and attendance at clinics.

I knew it was hopeless, I had remembered that from my nurse training. Sarcoma was treatable, but melanoma was a death sentence. Ma and I were in the know and we were keeping our patient in the dark.

'It doesn't sound good, Jude, does it?' he would say emerging from the specialist.

'Well, we'll just keep going. No one really knows,' Ma would reply.

Yet we both knew full well the prognosis. Even with her nursing knowledge some forty years out of date. We prepared ourselves for the worst with no protection at all, like falling and being unable to put your hands up to break your fall. We knew the hurt would come. There is relief when it finally happens, when the road comes to an end, when you reach the 'This is it' moment. How strange we humans are to find comfort in that.

I was pregnant with my first child when we learned of Pa's illness. As my pregnancy progressed, instead of listening to whale music or Mozart, the fads of the day, my unborn reverberated to the pulses of my guttural sobs. My body ached to the sounds of grief when it should have been singing to the joy of anticipation of new life.

As a nurse I had felt adamant about the sharing of prognoses. Where families pleaded with doctors not to come clean, I felt the patient had a right to know, not to be kept in the dark. It seemed to me a blatant violation of human rights and dignity. I would want to know. But I couldn't share my fears with him.

We were in despair of how little could be done. The cancer support sister in her short skirts and frilly blouses, more busty barmaid than motherly matron, was not who Ma wanted to support her through this. An easy repository for her anger, how dare she dress like that. Call herself a nurse? She didn't even look like one. And yet Pa remained stoically accepting throughout.

He lost weight and at his sixtieth birthday party I made a speech through the tears, handing over my nine-month-old boy to Ma so that I could concentrate on what I had to say. Everyone there knew he would be unlikely to celebrate his sixty-first birthday, but no one could gauge the rate of decline.

So we just celebrated the man we all loved. And Pa smiled through it all of the time.

He had been chirpy when we had visited him in hospital when he had his chemotherapy. Up until then the only time he had been an inpatient was when he had his appendix out. Perhaps that was the format he had in mind. Visitors come in bearing a bag of grapes, fielding questions about the hospital food and when you are coming home. I think he was playing the recovering patient for us, not looking too far ahead, taking one day at a time.

He came home from hospital having made a decision. He had had enough of the chemotherapy, it was more than he could bear. It made him feel like death. Listening to him explain his decision, I have never respected him more. He wasn't frightened of dying, just of leaving us girls behind, Ma, Caroline and me. We hugged him with all our might, wanting to pass on our strength to him, to make him well.

How did Pa cope? Not through talking. He prepared for the end through action, doing was his words, tying up the loose ends; painting the garage window frames in his anorak, the piercing winter chill cutting through his chemo-compromised body. To do as many of his jobs as he could, to buy time in that way – to get ahead of time. And so smoothing the transition of his allocation of jobs to Ma before he took his leave.

The last time I saw him at home he was sitting in his chair and I kissed him goodbye, a normal goodbye before setting off for my journey back to my home. I hovered at the door as I left the room, sensing I should be making more of it, but I couldn't. We just looked at each other knowingly. Maybe this was to be farewell, maybe it wasn't. A few days later he collapsed and slipped into the deep sleep of the coma from which he never awoke.

Arriving with the funeral cortège, Ma asked the vicar to tell the congregation that they were welcome to come back to the house for refreshments. He replied saying he didn't think that was a good idea. The church, Christchurch Priory where both Caroline and I were married and our children christened, was full to bursting. There wouldn't be room for them all.

How are you expected to sing at a funeral? It is hard enough to breathe let alone sing some ancient lyric. I gave up. I shut the hymnal. This was no time to stand on ceremony. This was a time to just be, to do what it took to survive the moment. There is comfort in friendships. The people who came like supporters of some relegated team for a final hurrah. You know who you are and I cherish you for that. And the ones who tried but couldn't make it, the flights and train schedules scuppering your heartfelt intentions. And to come to mourn at Christmas, the season of joy.

After he had gone, the smell of him lingered in his clothes, yielding memories, the joy, the laughter. That is what his clothes left behind. A closet full of jokes, optimistic and full of hope. It is their expectancy that kills – the pain that no one has told them he is not coming back. If Ma hadn't taken them to the charity shop, months later, they would still be there, awaiting his return. To begin with they were a comfort; open the closet and his presence is still there, the smell of him, the jumper to cuddle, proof that he had lived. But like Christmas decorations that feel so relevant when you are in the festive mood, they feel so uncomfortably out of place when you aren't.

Optimistic, warm-hearted, full of joy – sadness wasn't an emotion we associated with him, which is why it felt so difficult to comprehend. Think of Pa and your heart fills up and a big beaming smile gets drawn on your face. We never associated him with despair. Not until he had gone. But that was our emotion, not his.

Together we learned to cope. Retelling the stories about our shop days are what kept my family sane during those first few years without him. We never stopped speaking about him, of him, to him. We never pretended he was gone. In our deepest despair, when the walls were closing in, if we could just tell a story about him, we could feel close to him and turn our sadness to laughter. With eyes puffy and bloodshot from too much crying, we would find ourselves reliving over and over again the fun we had had from having him around.

'Do you remember the time he wore sandals to our Confirmation?' one of us would say.

'Yes.'

'We were all dressed up, ready to leave the house for the service, when he came downstairs in his light-coloured summer suit, shirt and tie, wearing sandals.'

'And Ma, you said, "Clive, you can't wear sandals to church."'

'And he replied, "Why not? Jesus did."'

'And then we all just looked at him in silence knowing it was so wrong but he was so right.'

Then we would laugh until our jaws ached, grateful for the relief.

We kept him alive in the only way we knew, by telling stories, repeating them over and over because, well, we didn't have any new ones. Constant retellings made us feel we could visit him whenever we wanted. Just think of him and feel the love. He became accessible again, like picking up the phone, but better than that, he was never out.

And that is what I have been doing here, retelling the stories, deepening my connection. We all lose someone, and nothing, no one, can prepare you for it. A broken heart hurts. And the blow is not softened even if you know it is coming. Putting up your guard is useless, but you live in hope.

When the conversation turned to regret, of his life cut short or the fact that his grandchildren would never know him, we soon learned there is no comfort there. Regret is a black hole; it has no silver lining. Gratefulness is the way forward out of grief. Through focusing on the fun times, the laughter, the hilarity of everyday events, we felt lucky, blessed, not mourners left behind.

Talking of him freely as an ongoing part of our lives, we did our best to carry on as normal. It helped set the tone for how other people treated us. Grief can drive even the closest friends away because they don't know what to say or how to behave. Are they frightened of making you feel worse? Talking of him showed that we didn't expect them to tiptoe around mentioning his name. If we could laugh about him, so could they.

Age and experience give a fresh perspective. Going back, things looked smaller than I recalled. My friends' huge rocking horse, the width of South Street, the size of the market, all seemed to have shrunk with my lack of attention. I suppose in the intervening years I have travelled and seen more things to compare them with.

It has been the same with my beliefs. With time I have been able to put them in perspective, to measure them against other things. At the time, I adopted them because I thought that was all there was. The pressure of expectation; this is what you believe, this is what you do. But now I see that there are choices. They never said that I could choose.

As a child I was taught that when people die they go to Heaven. They pass away, they leave your side and go to an inaccessible place. I would look up at the sky and think of all the departed souls floating around up there. The language is all about loss and departure. We had lost him, he had departed.

As with anything, it is not until you go through an experience that you realise what you feel about it. To begin with I adopted the belief patterns I had been taught. It was one of the hardest things I have ever asked myself to believe – that Pa had gone, that I would never be able to communicate with him again. It didn't sit comfortably with me. I struggled to believe it. It was the finality and inaccessibility that I couldn't cope with.

And then something happened that challenged that belief.

I had been staying with Ma, at the home she had shared with Pa, a couple of roads back from the sea near Bournemouth. It was about ten years since Pa had died. She had taken me to see a flat she wanted to buy. The flat was lovely, overlooking the sea and very well maintained. It seemed the ideal place for her to move to but it was a big step, downsizing from the house she had lived in with Pa, and she was worried about what he would think. Would Pa think she should move?

That was the thought on her mind as I was getting ready to depart. I got in the car, but as I was about to drive off I had a strong feeling that it wasn't time to leave. I needed to go for a walk, or rather, I needed to be taken for a walk. Without being able to explain it fully, I said to Ma that I couldn't leave just yet, and wanted to have another look at the sea.

I have felt a natural affinity with the sea all my life, perhaps because I grew up close to the coast. It always uplifts me and helps me feel grounded. As I headed off towards the beach, not quite sure of my direction, I assumed that I just wanted to sit on the beach again. But as I started off down the sea road I suddenly stopped walking in that direction and turned round to go towards the headland. When Pa died we had a memorial bench positioned in the most beautiful spot on Hengistbury Head. It overlooks the sea as well as Christchurch Priory, the church where he gave me away when I got married, where my sister got married and where both my children were christened, and where we held his funeral service. It is lovely to see people sitting there enjoying the view, although we were mortified one day when my daughter, then aged about four, told a couple, 'You can't sit there! That's my Grandpa's seat.'

I walked towards Pa's bench and as I approached I saw two women sitting there. I moved closer to eavesdrop on their conversation. They were talking about moving house and I heard one of the women say, ' . . . although I was worried about it, downsizing was the best thing I ever did. I love my flat, I love living here.'

I smiled. Of course Pa would want Ma to move to this flat. In fact, he would have liked to have lived there himself. I apologised for the intrusion and said that I couldn't help but overhear that one of them was downsizing. I explained that my mum was considering doing the same.

'Tell her to go for it,' the woman said. 'She won't regret it!'

I walked back to Ma's place to tell her what I had heard. I felt a bit embarrassed saying that I thought I had received a message from Pa, but that is what I believed.

From that day I have opened my mind to the fact that Pa has never left me. Would a parent ever leave the side of a child? Over the years I have nurtured this relationship and feel close to him in a way that is different from when he was alive. I believe he is around me and that I can draw him to me whenever I want. If I am ever anxious or confused, I pull him close and instantly feel safe. We used to go running together, although as a marathon runner his idea of a gentle jog was somewhat different to mine. I like to think of him running next to me, encouraging me to keep going.

Making sense of the world surely only comes with time. I have looked afresh, like opening up a grand old house that has been closed up and mothballed away. I have drawn back the shades and let in the light, and taken another look. What if he hadn't gone? Why would he go? If it was me instead of him, I wouldn't have left. I trust him to do the same. And that is when it began, the doubts, the questions over the existing beliefs, that departure from this life is final. Slowly I started to turn up my senses, to be aware, to trust my intuition and to breathe again, after what seemed like I had been holding my breath.

I am in a very different place from where I was as a child. I have tried on other people's beliefs for size and realised that many of them don't fit. If I have a sense that I am *trying* to believe something then I know it is not what I believe. I don't believe in the finality of life, that life is short, that life on earth is all you get. I believe we each have the wisdom and power to find our own truths.

Ultimately it is about trusting your intuition and listening to your heart. And that is something I am trying to do, every single day.

I have wondered what I have inherited from Pa, or through him, from someone further up the family track. What I would have liked to have had from him, but fear I have not, or at least not in the measure I would have liked, is not caring about what other people think. He had the drive to do things his way. His way was as good as any way.

We meet our parents in their adulthood, so I only have second-hand stories of what he was like as a child. Perhaps meeting them at this stage of their lives is the godsend it is meant to be, giving them time to iron out their childlike wants and ways, refining themselves before the responsibility of parenthood arrives. Perhaps that is why it is so hard as a daughter to think of your father as a child, cowering on the landing as his parents argued, kept awake, trying to sleep in the cold box room above the porch of the 1930s semi, Crittall windows concealed in condensation. No wonder he always hated those. Or as the small boy in shorts kicking a football, trying to grow and spread his wings with a short-tempered father who would argue for the sake of it, who filled his head with risks of what could go wrong over his potential to get things right. From where had he inherited that?

And yet they are still the same people as when they were children, some characteristics ironed out, chips and blocks perhaps picked up. They have the same passions and leanings, the same things that brought them joy as a child. Parents may appear old, but it is just a label we give them, to set them apart from ourselves; to distance them and justify our alternative ways of thinking at a time when we want to be different from them. The insights and experiences from another age, twenty, thirty years earlier, don't make them old, just more seasoned, experienced, broader-perspectived perhaps.

Pa emerged from childhood determined, stopping to ask his father for neither blessing nor advice, doing things his way. Acting with speed, with action as the verb requires, never inertia, never wasting time. Knowing the enjoyment of downtime and reward; a pint of beer and fistful of peanuts in front of a spaghetti western. The thrill of cars, perhaps that was his outlet. Where did the need for that passion come from? His mum, sporty and carefree until the osteoarthritis hit, and motherhood again at forty-three. The natural teenage urge for freedom, for freedom to do and to be, and to explore for oneself. And so the passion for cars, something he nurtured, built and raced, and passed on in part to me. But what else? What else are his gifts to me?

When Ma downsized and moved to her flat, she kindly gave me a few special things that I had grown up with around me. One of them is Pa's Vienna Regulator clock that dates from around 1890. I like its brass pendulum and weight, and its cream porcelain dial with pretty filigreed hands. It is not hard to see that a man who loved tinkering with cars would enjoy clocks, with their precision and harmonic tick. Its ticking was a constant at home that I never really noticed. When Pa died the clock stopped working. None of us remaining were privy to his specialised technique and know-how of keeping the thing going. So when it stopped, it stayed stopped. It had several long visits to a local clock mender who got it working again, but temperamentally.

Then Ma gave it to me. I found the most ideal clock mender through recommendation, a man who Pa would most likely have chosen himself. He had a gentleness that suggests a love and respect for clocks, adapting his van with bespoke wooden cases lined with a blanket in which to transport them. He did a thorough repair and overhaul of the clock for me and set it up on the wall. It has never stopped since. It is the most beautiful gift of Pa's that I could ever have. To me it is his heartbeat.

I lost him. I lost him when I was thirty-three and he was sixty. He was broken off from me like a piece of chocolate off my chocolate bar and I was left incomplete. I came with a bit missing, like a toy that no one wants. And that became my sense of identity, a misfit for a while, searching for the missing piece. For at least the first three years after he had gone. I hadn't wanted him to leave, though the warning signs were there. I knew it was coming, his leaving. I was preparing, but I wasn't prepared. Through convention I started talking about him in the past tense.

After he died I lost that feeling of invincibility that we had felt when we were together; a family unit, a pack of four. We weren't invincible, one of us had died. We were as vulnerable as everybody else. I was thrown off kilter, not just because of my grief, but because my self-identity no longer seemed relevant, my self-identity was of the past. With him gone, it was gone.

Identity is the story we tell ourselves. I can choose the things that define me, it is a choice not a given. Like someone listing their profession as a lawyer when they haven't practised for twenty years, or as a painter who no longer paints. But that person is the same, that experience never leaves them. It is as good a description as any. It reflects their life's aspirations, their dreams, the things of which they are most proud. It is true. It shows a glimpse of who they are on the inside, their character, that they got there, even if they are not there now.

Going back to the shop made me realise that nothing really had changed. The feeling of strength was still there. It had always been there, even when we were grieving its demise. The shop had gone, but the memories and tugs to my heart were as strong as when the shop was thriving. Going back to the shop I became heady on the essence of what had been. I had lifted the lid and found it smelt the same. While my disoriented eyes tried to recognise the shop as I had remembered it, despite the walls knocked down, the sweet jars gone, the cellar stairs concealed, my body knew. Like a parent reunited with a child after many years apart, I just knew.

I remain part of his story, even time cannot take that away. Like a sail that is let loose, flapping free, I choose to tighten the ropes, to harness the wind to propel me. His story is not lost, I keep it safe. And for those who never knew him, through reading this book, you have, I hope, a sense of him for yourself.

Afterword

It has been a beautifully cathartic process, researching and writing this book, getting back in touch with people from my childhood, my teens, my home town, gleaning snippets of memories that I had missed. As I got closer to the end, it became clear to me that I wanted to publish it under my maiden name of Osmond. It is a book about my family, about Osmond's, and so, putting that name on the front cover as the author made sense. When it came to the practicalities, I realised that I didn't want the confusion of having a pen name and a real name. I felt excited about the prospect of changing it permanently, recapturing that sense of belonging to my family name, to Pa's name. He used to joke that in having two daughters, the name would not pass on. Perhaps there was a sense of responsibility, a desire to keep the name alive, the name that links him to me. So, after twenty years of calling myself by my married name of Lucinda Slater, I changed my name by Deed Poll and reclaimed my maiden name. What has amazed me is how beautiful a feeling it is to be reconnected with the name of my birth. I realised how much I had missed it.

Grandma's poem

THE LITTLE THINGS

It's the little things that count in life,
A sunny smile, no words of strife,
Days to prove just one good deed,
A helping hand to friends in need.
As we travel on through the years,
We get the sunshine, and share the tears.
Friends come and go in life we see,
Time heals the wounds, but holds the key.
To memories stored for rich and poor,
Which often makes the heart feel sore.
Things we planned did not come true,
It happens daily to me and you.
Years roll on, how quick they fly,
And often bring a tear, a sigh.
Count your blessings as they go,
Fate decides it should be so.

Marjorie Bunt

Pa's diary

The following is the only entry in a handwritten diary that Pa wrote for my son Sam, and his as then unborn grandchildren, my daughter Sophia, and my nephews Joel and Ben. I was keen for them, and any later additions to the family, to have a first-hand account of Pa's early life because I knew so little about it. Sadly it is the only entry because by the time Pa wrote it, he was very ill and had little energy to write.

I was born on 17th August 1937 in Bromley Hospital, Kent, in the evening. I don't know how much I weighed. My father said that as my mother had big hips she had easy births. Both my parents were 30 years old when I was born. My first name was chosen so that it could not be shortened. I don't know where my second name came from.

We lived at 74 Repton Road, Orpington, Kent. We stayed there for twenty-six years. The house was built in 1933, a semi-detached three bedroom house typical of that period. My bedroom was the box room over the porch, very cold in winter! No heating!! We had a long garden with a railway embankment at the bottom, the trains went from London to Dover.

My earliest memories are of me in a pedal car going round the back garden, this was my favourite toy. Both my parents played a lot of tennis and my father also played semi-professional football as a centre forward so I was encouraged to kick a ball around and hit tennis balls up against the wall of the house.

I was only two when the Second World War started.

My first bicycle was a Fairy Cycle which had been handed down from a neighbour who had an older boy called Tony. I had this when I was about four. I can remember waiting in the porch for the all clear siren to sound after an air-raid then I would pedal off to school.

My tennis racket also a hand down from Tony, his family belonged to the same tennis club as my parents, Goddington Sports Club.

I have two sisters, Jean (three years younger) and Valerie (thirteen years younger). We all enjoyed playing cards with our parents and usually around Christmas time we played a lot of blow football and table tennis on the dining room table. My mother used to get so excited playing blow football, the ball went everywhere!

My parents were keen gardeners and so to encourage us we were given patches of our own to look after.

PERISHED IN HEAVY SEA

SHOCK FOR HOLIDAYMAKERS AT CORNISH BEACH

The holiday crowd at Spit beach, near Par, was shocked yesterday when the rumour that a young man had been drowned there soon after 1 p.m. was confirmed.

An eye-witness, Mr. Arthur Phipps, of Bodmin, a visitor, said that he heard a shout, and saw a man in the water waving his arms. He saw a man go out to the rescue of the bather, who subsequently proved to be Mr. Fred. Bullock, of Okewoon, near Bugle.

It transpired that Bullock, a single man, aged 26, and Henry Higman, of Bugle, went bathing. A heavy sea was running, and the tide was ebbing. Both got into difficulties, but Higman managed to reach the shore. Mr. Alfred Blight, of Mount Charles, St. Austell, told a "Western Morning News" representative that he saw a hand above the water about 300 yards out, and he swam out towards it. When he reached the spot there was no sign of Bullock. He remained in the water about half an hour, but without result.

Henry Higman, the other bather, said that Bullock was the better swimmer, but he went further out. He (Higman) got in difficulties, but managed to get ashore.

The police, under Sergt. Prout, of Tywardreath, organized a search along the cliffs from Par to Point Gribben, near Fowey, as it is believed that the current will take the body over towards these cliffs, unless it has lodged in the numerous rocks round the beach.

Spit beach, though small, is very popular, and has always been described as a safe beach, but yesterday it was agreed that it was dangerous to venture far out at that spot with a heavy sea running.

TWO HOLIDAY TRAGEDIES

BOATING FATALITY AT EXETER

BATHER DROWNED IN CORNWALL

CLIFF ADVENTURE AT NEWQUAY

Tragedy intruded into the Bank-holiday gaiety in the West, two deaths by drowning occurring yesterday.

One was at Exeter, where a young married man perished through the capsizing of a rowing boat on the River Exe within sight of a crowd of holidaymakers, while there was a bathing fatality at Spit Beach, near Par, a young man getting into difficulties in the heavy sea, which was running at the time, and being seen no more. A companion also got into difficulties, but managed to get ashore.

A young man and woman had an

Fred's reported drowning

These are two newspaper cuttings reporting Fred's drowning at Par Beach, Cornwall on Bank Holiday Monday, 4th August 1930. The extracts are from *The Western Morning News and Mercury*, Tuesday 5th August, 1930 and *The Cornishman and Cornish Telegraph*, Thursday 7th August, 1930.

Acknowledgements

Survival rates for malignant melanoma have improved, especially in the last five years and there is much hope for the future with the arrival on the scene of immunotherapies which are having a major and positive impact on the treatment of this previously hard-to-treat disease.

I have tried to recreate events and conversations from memory. Some names, identifying characteristics and details have been changed to protect the privacy of individuals or for literary effect.

I would like to thank the following people:

My mentor Ros Barber for helping me believe that I could write a book, and getting me to do it, Tamsin Shelton for her sensitive and perceptive editing, Peter O'Connor for the striking cover design, Nici Holland for her careful and skilled formatting, and helping make this such a special book for me, Emma Davies and Karen de Snoo for help with images, and archivists at the Dorset County Museum and Dorset History Centre for assisting with research.

Friends and family and all those who have contributed time and encouragement. In particular, Clare Grassby, my cheerleader and school friend who read it first, Susan Ridley who read it and loved it, and like me, has a Grandma called Marjorie, Suzanne Douglas for her incredible eye for detail, Rick Rogers for telling me I'm good at maths, Nigel Waters for pointers on publishing, and members of Guildford Speakers Club for being a testing ground for these stories.

Heartfelt thanks go to the people who have shared their stories and allowed me to use their anecdotes: Stuart and Rita Turner, John True, Pam and Peter Seaton, Kate, Sarah, Vicky and Nicko, Jean Moleta, Val Millen, Catherine Duran Le Roy and Francis Duran, Jean Pierre and Lucienne Le Roy. Stupot (you know who you are) for giving me my first favourite book, Tim Whitefield (first seen in aviator sunglasses, white T shirt and blue jeans) and Bill and Vera Jesty for sharing their knowledge of Thomas Hardy.

All the customers of Osmond's down the years, and to our very special 'shop girls', Julie Plummer (née Lacey), Irene Bishop, Bertha Eyres, Janet, Mrs. Denis and Mrs. Faye. And to our fellow shopkeepers and shop assistants in Dorchester. Thank you all for being part of this story.

My daughter Sophia for expert critiquing and for capturing the elusive words that escaped me, my son Sam, an author in the making, for his wit and encouragement. My husband Mark for topping up my self belief and never doubting for a moment that I would see this to the end. Also, for selling copies of this book before it had even been published.

Ma for the stories and the laughs, and patience at my constant questioning, and my sister Caroline, author in waiting. Ma, you said we could write a book. Well, here it is. Caroline, it's your turn next.

And finally, Pa, for being a smiling, loving presence in my life.

About the author

Lucinda Osmond grew up in Dorchester, working with her dad in 'the shop' on Saturdays and in the holidays. She left Dorchester aged eighteen to follow her childhood dream to become a nurse, and later became a lawyer. She is happy to have at last put down on paper the stories she has been carrying around in her head for years. She is married with two children and although now lives in Surrey, remains a Dorset girl at heart.

If you enjoyed A Sweet Life, please consider leaving a review:

www.amazon.co.uk
www.amazon.com
www.goodreads.com

Connect with Lucinda online:

Twitter @lucinda_writes
Facebook lucindawrites
www.lucindawrites.com
lucinda@lucindawrites.com

Lightning Source UK Ltd.
Milton Keynes UK
UKOW05f1832300617
304450UK00001B/4/P